AGENDA

CH01432806

CONTENTS

2

Editorial

I hope you enjoy this issue which marks a return to mainly UK (and Ireland) issues, and to the traditional black and white covers for the pocket-sized journals.

The important Irish poet, Pádraic Fallon, is quoted at some length in this issue's *Notes for Broadsheet Poets* from his 'Poet's Journal' in the recently published book, *A Poet's Journal & Other Writings, 1934–1974* (The Lilliput Press, Dublin 2005). He comments that a poet should have 'eyes for even the tiniest wordfall' and go on to 'live in his hearers': the aims, surely, of the poets included here.

Pádraic Fallon states: 'The poem finds the poet'. Similarly, here, the poems on the theme of water seem to have found this issue and shaped it of their own accord, giving this section that 'personality' which Fallon accords to the most interesting books.

In fact, these poems on water, and more specifically those on the sea, seem an extension of *The Sea! The Sea!*, a wonderful anthology of poems about the sea edited by Peter Jay, and published by the Anvil Press in October 2005.

This is a must-have treasury whose water music moves with the 'swing of the sea'. It includes old favourites traditionally learnt by rote, remarkable little known translations from Old English, Latin, Spanish, Irish, Italian, Norwegian, Serbo-Croat, Russian, Bengali, French (translated mostly by Peter Dale, former Associate Editor of *Agenda*, and by Harry Guest, a frequent *Agenda* contributor), and some very familiar but not often anthologised poems. For example to my delight I found here: 'A Life on the Ocean Wave' by Epes Sargent (1813–1880) sung to his squeeze-box by my father who, as a Captain in the Royal Navy, dedicated the main part of his life to the sea, and even the hymn 'Eternal Father Strong to Save' by William Whiting (1825–1878) that I and my two sisters chorused passionately 'for those in peril on the sea'.

There are a couple of omissions, perhaps. One has to be Wallace Stevens' sonorous, colourfully-patterned poem, 'Sea Surface Full of Clouds', which captures 'the slopping of the sea' with such lines as: 'The gongs rang loudly as the windy booms/ Hoo-hooed it in the darkened ocean-bloom', and 'An uncertain green/ Piano-polished, held the tranced machine/ of ocean, as a prelude holds and holds' ... The other omission is at least an excerpt or two from Hopkins' superbly memorable 'Wreck of the Deutschland'. After all, who summons better the texture, power, taste, feel and energy of the 'cobble-fleeced foam', that 'rash smart sloggering brine' with such examples as 'And the sea flint-flake, black-

3

backed in the regular blow' whose 'Wiry and white-fiery and whirlwind-swivellèd snow/ Spins to the widow-making unchilding unfathering deeps'? However, presumably these two great poems either were sacrificed because of choice or did not fit into Peter Jay's stipulation that any poem selected had to have 'the sea as its main background or scene (real or implied), motivating circumstance, pivotal image or symbol'. Hence he settled for Wallace Stevens' equally impressive 'The Idea of Order at Key West', and for Hopkins' short poem 'Heaven-Haven'.

The next issue of *Agenda* will be another general issue, to enable the appearance in print of the patient poets who have been queuing up. Future plans include a 'Reconsideration of Rilke' issue and a 'Women Only' issue, interspersed with general issues, each with a special focus.

Thanks are given to all contributors, including to those waiting to appear in *Agenda*, and to subscribers/readers for being those 'hearers'.

Patricia McCarthy, Editor
Marcus Frederick (Fred), Admin.

VISIT THE WEBSITE
www.agendapoetry.co.uk
FOR AN EXTRA SUPPLEMENT OF ESSAYS,
BROADSHEET 6 FOR YOUNG VOICES
(and artists),
NEWS, POEMS AND TRANSLATIONS

New essays online:

Young Broadsheet Essayist: Michael Kinsella

Julia Forster: Critical Openness: A Study of Poetry in Public Places

Translations include:

The Turkish poet, Guven Turan, translated by Ruth Christie

Translations from the French of Samaine Bouinou, Hervé Chesnais, Julien Payan by Fred Johnston

Translations from the Irish of Séan O'Ríordáin by Greg Delanty

More 'Water' poems, including:

David Betteridge's 'Found' – a sequence

Alex Smith

Voyages

Scenes from Pericles

I

Thaisa

i

Childbirth at sea

Pericles' issue and bloodline:

the blood and water flowing
in the scream of the storm;

against the lurch and strain
a palimpsest
of indelible stain
on the ship's boards,

Thaisa's body racked
against racked timbers,
frame against frame
to the point of brasting

then sudden and malignant calm –
both ship and woman
drifting, insensible.

ii

Sea Burial

Muscles and sinews strain
to the heft and pull of ropes
as they lift, then lower
the coffin gently
as though it contained
a live and precious cargo
entrusted to their care –

breathless and panting
they align to the ship's motion,

a rocking to rhythms of grief.

iii

At the Temple

Diaphanous, the silvered light
from off Thaisa's hair:

folding the altar cloth with care
she smoothes each crease
with fine white hands.

Her silence filled with sorrow,
she glides through the sanctuary,
touching each vessel
through rehearsals of love

and, at ceremony's end,
lifts up her eyes –
twin olive lamps – in trust.

Marina

i

The abduction

A cold dryness
in the mouth,
in the eye,
the body frozen

as though marble or bronze,
rigid in attitude,
ears turned to stone:

running and shouting
along the beach,
just fifty yards away
when she notices a gull
landing awkwardly on a roof,
shuffling its feet forward
to keep balance.

The evening sky flares
to a blooded abstract,
impasto, throbs
to a pulse in the brain
that blots out the coastline
and the embracing sea.

Escape

She thought a brothel
was a soup kitchen
and stews a dish of orts;

thus filched and bargained for,
she added quickly to her definitions:
if she did not escape
her life would be
the history of her body.

She holds her breath, closes
the door gingerly and,
step by cautious step,
makes her way into fresh
intrusions of weather,
observes tearing clouds,
the timeless shore.

Seascape, with frieze of girls

They enter from the promenade
flushed with racquet exercise,
fall onto couches, laughing.

Chiaroscuro: sunlight floods
from the arbour, scatters
green and yellow coins about the room.

Rituals of hospitality
announce a cliché of sounds:
the ordered rattling of plates and flasks,
short crescendos of social laughter.

A gaiety of strings and pipes:
music unifies,
binds the discontinuous.

As the last notes resonate
among garden statuary
she reflects on changes possible
within so short a time.

The room chills, a salt breeze
enters the open casement,
flecks her skin.

III

A Villanelle for Pericles

Every voyage is a voyage of loss
and mariners craft a sombre farewell.
Each ocean's a grave we venture to cross.

We sailed our tall barques from Tarsus to Kos
and witnessed comrades sinking in the swell.
Every voyage is a voyage of loss.

Our prow became a funereal boss,
more dead than alive, we journeyed through hell.
Each ocean's a grave we venture to cross.

We wish for a tomb roofed over with moss,
not the sea-fog alarm sounding our knell.
Every voyage is a voyage of loss.

I cling to trinkets that others count dross,
cheap bracelets and rings, a sea-urchin shell.
Each ocean's a grave we venture to cross.

We aren't deceived by El Dorado's gloss,
there's more honesty in the tocsin bell.
Every voyage is a voyage of loss.
Each ocean's a grave we venture to cross.

IV

Unification of Pericles, Thaisa and Marina

We observe them through glass,
silent and holding hands,
cool, expressionless:

daughter, mother,
husband and father,
sea-swallowed, sea-borne
and sea-returned;

holding each to each,
they are indissoluble,
a single form cut in ivory
tinctured with the pearl of day.

June English

Retrospect

Whiffen Spit, Vancouver Island, 1966

I see you now,
black curly hair, leopard eyes,
on the harbour side of the lonely spit,
chain-smoking Players Weights,
with an eye on your watch...

I see you now,
in your red-check shirt,
your lumberjack boots,
kicking dried cuttlefish, scuttling crabs,
near a swarm of wasps on a squashed apricot.

I see you now,
fag in hand, skimming stones,
when our youngest was stung,
when he screamed with pain,
when he wet his pants.

I see you now,
standing cool and unmoved –
while I cleaned him up,
and we cleared away –
like a bit part actor in a boring play.

Family Day, June 1967

A picnic on the beach
at Whiffen Spit, you and me,
a chance to build those bridges,
the ones that Father Fahey
talked about, but never opened up . . .

Our sons paddling in rock pools,
excited by seaweed and snails;
me, with my arms around them,
calling, *See what we've found.*
That expectant moment, carved in memory
when the world spun and you stood still . . .

The picnic, laid out in Tupperware:
brown-bread sandwiches, prawn and tuna,
Black Forest Gateaux and fruit salad.
Little one shouting, *Come and get it.*
A timeless second, scanned to history,
the offered plate still hanging there . . .

The three of us, huddled together, kissing
and comforting, empty, alone.
Our eldest bringing the bag,
helping me through in his grown-up way.
Wanting you with us, not daring to ask,
fearing the words you didn't speak . . .

You on the Harbour side,
in camera. Unapproachable
as the Bald Eagle,
warily stripping the flesh
from a beached Chinooks Salmon.
Ready to fly . . .

Thanksgiving, October 1970

You at Whiffen Spit, on the seaward side,
where the Cascade mountains rise
in sheeted skies, like the demented
ghosts of wedding cakes and hawks
and turkey vultures flay the air.

Too quiet, our children's play in this
graveyard of the sea. Pensive,
they sift the bleached bones of cuttlefish
and conch, find a calcified starfish,
ask me why it doesn't swim.

You move to the harbour side, examine
sheltered rock pools, where small fish
dart and hide in seaweed gardens,
find a sea anemone, a pulsating cell, yielding
as the vulva and poke it with a stick.

Later, in the shell called home,
you strip me, tie me, throw me down,
kneel between my lilied knees,
thrust screwdrivers into my womb,
withdraw, stand back, then click and flash . . .

The rape recorded in that photograph,
(retained by you, purpose unknown),
reversed the light and shade in me,
stamped *jelly fish* on my psyche:
skewered the woman from the girl.

David Cooke

Shire song

Was it the calm sunlight
Of his going – the drowned boy
Singing through the shires,
Who down lane whistled
And reeled some blood song
Which filled and flattered
These bones that they
Might again live!

He was a fisher of sorts.

Death makes one real,
Was the motto sewn
Inside his coat.
           He could reel
In his line having caught
A cold or speckled trout.
Yet his voice in cadence
Hummed a vision of his toil.

Sing me grief or sing me
Rain on the river.

His bright fettered song
Tethered and snapped the air,
Then drifted downriver,
Until almost – as sun went
Under, he became a rare
Scatter of wings, some wild
Goose which took flight where
Darkness rose upon water.

Michael Kirkham

Siren Song (1984)

Today, playing truant from himself, he plays
his daughter's music, Elton John's
plangent *Sad Song*. The drowse and swing,
the sweet-talking of guitars, the soft
piston-thump of drum, the high-flung
hammer-voice with anvil clang
beating into shape a pliant sense:
it's a potent mix, has the kick of a horse.

Coaxing, folksy, a salesman's pitch
(weren't we all spawned in the same dark ditch?)
it says: Trust me – I am loud, I contain
multitudes. It croons: Seek solace
in this brew of travelled wisdom:
'When all hope is gone, turn on
the sad songs, turn 'em on,
the sad songs *say* so much' . . . and such
– a sequined siren call to let all
go; a sanctifying unction makes it
sweetly sick. And you're hooked all right –
one bite, you're drugged and dragged along:
compulsive lullabying sad song.

Today, in deliberate debauch
of self, he plays his daughter's music.

Peter Abbs

Against Creation

After *Dante's Inferno*: Canto xxvi

Master, I said, if within these flames this man can speak,
Let me draw close to hear his words. And Virgil replied:
Listen and Ulysses will tell you how and where he died.

The oval flame began to flicker and then stretch higher
As if the inferno's wind was slowly rising. Then from the fire
I heard a spectral voice. When I escaped the wiles of Circe

Nothing could keep me. Neither my son, nor my father,
Least of all my doting wife. An inner daimon drove me on
To crack the riddle of the sphinx, to take seductive nature

To the rack and screw. How I longed to map the dark streams
Of the mind, break open the hieroglyphs of dreams,
Extract the recalcitrant code of matter, good or evil –

What did that matter? So I set out with a motley crew
And moved from place to place – Spain, Morocco, Sardinia,
And other slack backwaters where no-one spoke a word

Of Greek. Then I took my men to the edge of the known world,
Where maps end, where all pilots feel a deep unease
And turn their vessels back. Not me. My crew stared mutinous.

Seafarers, I said, we have come a long way to reach
This place which marks the beginning of uncharted seas
And we are ageing now. There's not a young man here.

So in whatever time remains – let us become as gods.
We were not born to live like beasts tethered to the fields
But to track down the source of power. To live dangerously!

My words calmed my fractious man. They clapped
As if it was some after-dinner speech, not an act of defiance
Against the odds. Together they bent to lift the heavy oars

And lunged with a new elation. For five days we rowed –
Until at night we could not read the configuration of the stars.
Then on the sixth day a rock came drifting through the haze.

Its bulk amazed. It was larger than anything I had ever seen.
I do not know why, one of the crew laughed hysterically.
It seemed the climax of our quest, this black barren screen

Blocking our progress. And then from nowhere a storm blew up.
It smacked our boat. Three times we spun around – the mast
Cracked and snapped, the prow reared up and then went down –

And over our reeling heads the water swirled and closed.

Ian Caws

Mill Water

I can't remember what we were saying
But it's gone now in the sound of water.
And a blackbird we stopped for on the bridge
Has taken his song where there is seeing
But nothing heard in the mill water's rush.
The water tells me to wait till later;
The water tells me there is no message
And nothing in its heart but a silence,
A clean obliteration in its wash
Of all that will be or that happened, once.

In the mill water there is only now
And now is forever, not mine to hold.
There are lips around me that are moving
But what they say is neither old nor new
And anyway, it's lost in the water,
Where pain dies and everything is healed,
Where nothing matters and there is loving
Without its complication and yearning
Stops for what should be better or sweeter.
The blackbird has flown; the wheel keeps turning.

Martin Cook

Winkling

Noise was somewhere else,
except for wind hints and gull calls,
when we sought the estuarine calm
of mudflats at Malltraeth,
where Tunicliffe depicted
curlew, redshank, brent geese
and a motley of sea birds
in delicate line and colour.

A bearded, care-lined man in black shoes
squelched across the mud flats.

His sleeves were rolled up above his elbows,
nautical tattoos festooned his arms,
and he scrabbled among seaweed and stones for winkles,
plunging each small mollusc into a pocket.

He turned and talked about the tides
and an impending weather change.

We left the foreshore, walking quickly,
and secured our cottage windows with undue care.

Nicholas Jagger

Sail Maker

He had told me of the goods off-loaded
in each of the docks, their high-Victorian names.
Of the bombers they had run from
during the war, and of their fear under fire.

Later, I followed his spoken map,
walking across thin-soiled ground
that offered weed-bouquets to that past:
to the skeletal sheds and shacks,
piles of silvered timber, landlocked craft.

One day in bright winter,
I walked unchallenged on to a wharf,
and berthed there in silence
were monuments to a war more recent:
rusted trawlers, the furthest out of eye-reach.

Instead of paint were massive autumn tints,
brilliant against clear sky, two lines of orange
receding to a distant sea no longer their lawful
kingdoms, and I intruding there.

I could walk no further, and still more boats
were slipping under eighth-hour dusk unseen,
and still he called me on.

Lawrence Sail

Putting Out to Sea

For Erica and Oli

Grand though it is, the view from the tilted headland
over the horseshoe of the bay, where the moon arranges
the waters in a shifting hem of frill and foam
tide after tide, it divulges little of the ship
slipping its mooring today, as we watch. And yet,
even without a bill of lading, we can surely
guess at some of the cargo – a sense of humour
nicely salted, for instance; a blue and white scarf,
endless recipes, wine for the wine-dark sea.

Every marriage, you could say, keeps its open secret
under wraps and is, as are some poems, de-
cipherable only with its own key. And look –
here comes the sea-wind scudding across the water,
inky and urgent, to brace and careen the hull,
making the compass spin in its bright binnacle,
making the most of the quick moment. And how
eagerly, as we look on, the ship puts out,
rewarding us with another real dream of happiness.

Double Portrait

By the long shore, this image of the mind
is turned inside out – the poet lies
back, one arm across his face
to ward off the obvious glare, amid
the windswept marram-grass that seethes
like a neural fever:
                    and the muse sits
alert, with hands clasped round her knees,
smiling from under the brim of her cap.
Patient, calm, she is waiting again
for a line to be thrown from an incoming boat,
ready as always to take up the slack.

John Torrance

Nocturne

Old shipwrecks cry revenge
to those who wake past midnight.
The doggers churn and churn
between the breakers and the cliff.

Up here, tonight, no more than a lullaby
sung by the hills to the sea
as it rolls in its bed.

Your breathing beside me
caresses the air.

Ah, but who dares
look down the drop of the years
into that wrecking-ground?

The Blue Pool

It burns more green than blue
and then again more blue than green,
antinomies of light
suspended, alternate
opaque and limpid, ardent, cool,
ice-blue and molten jade.

The stillness hums.
I breathe the sunwarmed resins
of aromatic pines.

So tell, blue-darting damsel-flies,
can a man be like an opal,
hospitable to contraries,
a bowl of brilliant shades?

Boscombe Pier

The pier-head theatre's like a brownfield site,
a factory past repair. Red placards voice
the risks of superannuated life –
THIS END UNSAFE (I know, I'm already there)
DANGEROUS DO NOT ENTER (alas, we have no choice).

Yet there are harmonies here between the soft
sea sloshing through the beams of rotting woodwork
and the cou-rou-cou of pigeons on the roof,
truant street-performers playing at gannets
who make of this asbestos slope their own Bass Rock.

Above the padlocked doors, grey-painted letters
spell out its name: this morgue of standup jokes
long fallen flat was called THE MERMAID once.
What things have we seen done at the Mermaid!
No, good Master Beaumont, not here, among these folks.

Though I can dream that prying moons might yet
wake midnight echoes on these boards, and dare
some amateur Prospero, risen from the 'fifties,
to tell the ever-clapping waves once more
'Our actors were all spirits, and are melted into air'.

Janice Fixter

A More Fluid Way of Being

Driving past a sign that offers
sea shimmer plants for sale,

we do not stop to ask, but wonder
if these plants always remember

the language of ocean.
Through granite, sandstone, basalt,

volcanic-hardened lava flows,
emotional geology,

we learn that roads must bend and curve
through shale and landslip,

that we exist between rock
and rock.

We pull off road
to glittering sea. Ripples

remind us of a more fluid way of being –
quicksilver light and water.

Gannets dive and plunge,
sparks of sun falling from the sky.

Nigel Jarrett

Tsunami

We never knew where you were,
Sumatra; now, you have moled
Into the lawn, destroying
Our nice view: yellow jasmine,
Fields of promising winter wheat,
The lane searched by sunsets.

Sumatra – you reminded us of
Anahorish in your lightness of consonant;
Your ironed-out syllables
Flattened everything to silence;
We gaped at your good fortune,
Tongued your sweet food from trees.

But, Sumatra, you carried a portent:
Your land is a beached raft of the Medusa,
Though 'Su' is the lightest of zephyrs
And 'matra' a double benediction.

Teach us your old lesson, Sumatra –
Something soothing, some mantra.

Killed on the Ice

is a verdict we were always being given
to explain the fates of the missing.
We saw them mock-courageous among the floes,
playing their games of catch-as-catch-can
until black lightning flailed them backwards,
their cries for help mimed in the distance.

But we knew their timidity, their trepidation,
how they would call us to the waterfront
and, barred by the wonders of rigor –
its machinations in the depths, its congealing power –
point to the first thrusting crystals on the ebb
then, upstream at an angle, the blocked trajectories.

27

Robert Blaney

El Nino

We gathered on the cliff
and rain descended like sea eagles
punching water.

We thought we knew her rhythms
but she had tricked us with her dirty secret,
the bringer of bounty and famine
returning after years of exile
like an apparition.

The child brought presents;
shoals of vapour sprouted giant cacti
and greened the volcanoes.
She made hummingbirds sing,
wild goats grow fat
but when the sea turned black
rivers of mud like lizards escaped
and ran through the town.

We put on masks, stood on the reef,
broke bread and drank wine,
and exchanged rings with the ocean.

The albatross abandoned its nest,
a wave of rats devoured its eggs
and sea lions grew as thin
as shreds of wet suits.

After the third week
the sea emptied of plants,
fish turned to coral
and the sea emptied of colour
and as we waited for the seasons to turn
the fishermen hauled up their nets
and sailed away.

Keith McFarlane

Storytelling

For Rosemary

To see again Aegean's wild, with twelve
close friends by night, calls back Odysseus,
these twenty years denied his domicile
by warring gods' great might.
                      See there the peerless
tapestry that's unpicked thread for thread,
and bright the unseen olive whose branches
made their bed. Let loose the flashing arrow
that twelve axe-heads struck through;
                      and see the brightness
in our hearts for all that gods can do.

For here is the power of story, and here
is the power of love, and here is the world
as ever it was before the primal
flood. For the power that rests in the eldest
of stones is the power that wakens in blood,
that remembers the songs, that remembers
the words that fire, that thunder, still in us.

Evenstar

For Artémis

You touch a place, close, by my heart
Where, this I promise you, no dark
Shall fall, though earth's blind teeming dim
And fail: the smallest flame holds back
The night, and shadows counterpoint
The fire we forge in blood and brain,
As lamps at sunset presage dawn
Though, one by one, the stars go out.

No rock might bear in obstinacy
Or faith greater resilience
Than this that love can steel from flesh
And gentleness; like water quenching
Flame, or ocean's patience shaping
Stone: each pulse-beat wakened dares
Become sublime, though synapse part,
And voice be broken, stilled by time.

John Greening

Eglwys Llangwyfan

Surrounded at high tide, and still used
for worship during high season, 'the church-
in-the-sea', where we stand congratulating

ourselves on one calm sunrise after Friday's
scourging breakers. These three have spelt
their names in clam and cockle on the rocky steps

that climb up to St Gwyfan's. They have
the old religion, but – to the oystercatchers' orange
warning hwyl – I feel the tug of an older

beneath eight centuries, beyond their shells,
that this stony path across the strand
leads west to, where a name in the turf

unnests a long-drowned Londoner.

Hiraeth

the long hurt

In the kitchen she extemporised laments on a penny whistle,
Give Me Your Hand and When the Tide Comes In,
as her grandmother leant on the dry-stone wall and cried
to the thistles across the land, to the church-in-the-sea.

Greg Delanty

Translations from the Irish of Seán O'Ríordáin (1916–1977)

Clifftop, Dunquin, August 1970

Prose Poem

This locality is saying something. If it could be put in words then it would be known that this locality was saying something. The sea, the rocks, the grass, everything growing here says this is the way it is. The people say it. They are silent saying it. It is what they say whether speaking or silent. Although it is not what they say. It would be a relief to hear it flushed out in words. It would be nothing new to us. It's said so forcefully by this locality that it must be examined from time to time. It is endurance.

The Start

(from a sequence)

There's a rumour of saints everywhere.
The wind is threading the air.
An ancient prayer slips memory.
My thoughts are blown astray once more.

Here in the pen of saints' reflections
a new image leaps to mind:
the song of a bird
showering scorn on life.

The music the bird pours forth
is his own island world; everyone
is granted an island of their own.
Those who ignore that shore haven't a prayer.

Gerard Smyth

Nora Barnacle's House

I was looking for Nora Barnacle's house
but never found it.
Instead I saw her apparition in the water
with the Corrib swan,
the one leading the others forward,
the one with slender contours
eyeing the stranger on the riverbank
under the flowering tree.

I was looking for the house of Nora Barnacle
but wandered instead up the aisle
of the stone-walled cathedral,
where liturgical smoke lingered
after some ritual, after the sign of peace
when everyone leaves to go out
into the other world where first
their eyes adjust and then they see
the choppy Corrib, the swan in the water,
and between the branches of the tree
petals falling, settling
on the grassy bank beside the weir.

Gary Allen

Lambeg

A well-aimed spit will break the tension,
split the head.

This rolling thunder raises the blood:
licking flames on faggots of sticks –

let the Spanish look to themselves
rock and gale will turn the tide

and singe the hair of confessor
or Virgin Queen –

allegiance is the Lord's preserve
and every soul his humble altar.

I knew a man who bred his own goats
among the high ground of a boggy field:

his skinning knife honed and whetted just so
the hide stretched on wooden frames –

he clothed the Cock of the North
but could turn his coat to an Irish beat.

Bring them down to these summer lanes
tarpaulin covered from country halls

each boasting of battles and honours won
Jericho-like they ring the hills

the linen mills, the weighted flax,
the beaten skins singing of war.

Missing

Bury my bones by the sea
at a lonely strand
where none of mine have ever been:

on dull days, lovers park their cars
to look at the crazy waves –

let dogs find me.

I am sixties concrete and stone
high-rise flats, elevated walkways –

my neighbours come to see me
they bring rope and hurley sticks.

I know how the ocean can smash ships –

oh listen to the slam of wood on flesh
iron jarred into open wounds,

and always the mournful singing of the wind.

All my priests are cowards
they fear the word of God –
no bell will ring for me

but lovers will walk the heavy sands
their heels tug upon my womb
their whispered love my absolution.

Kim Lasky

Kalypso

I

We talked, agreed you should return to her,
Years late but in time to make amends,
Weave some tale of trickery. On nectar
And ambrosia we fed, parting friends.
Then I gave myself to hunger, bared
Breasts for your fingers, legs for your tongue
More lavish than any marital bed.
I could claim coercion, but that would be wrong.
I wanted it, that one final pleasure,
My body unwrapped, your convenience.
I throbbed, full of you; knowing how later,
Sleeping with her, I would fever your dreams.
She might think me a whore for that,
But a whore knows to ask the
Price of a heart.

II

Afterwards sea-storm gusted the cypress
Warm as your breathing, as in the easy
Intimacy of leaving you confessed
The green fear, found tears at last for me.
Such nights are lost to the constellations
Now, with you lying safe in Ithaka,
Called home by the tug of a wife's patience;
The tongue that licks the wounds I healed for her.
At dusk I light cedar logs for company.
Through sleepless nights I burn to forget
As red embers fade into blue, willing
New indifference to snuff you out:
As if I'd never seen the weakness in you,
Never tasted the salt on your skin.

III

Mornings, I watch the constant sun spin her
Light into wine-dark waves, promising
Another day. At noon I take shelter
Held by a hollow cave. Cool evenings
I walk the settling copse, alone, relaxed,
All shipwrecks forgotten – until I come
Upon green alders where, with adze and ax,
I had him fell a boat to sail back home
To stubborn patience. No, not so stubborn;
Just a widow yet to learn she lost
Her man carelessly to another woman.
Waking from dreamless sleep I think of that,
Wonder if those missing years haunt her,
How often she regrets his return.

Lynne Wycherley

Shetland Lace

Time clings to a wisp of light –
spindrift, hairstreak, salt-spray.
The spindle lisps, the treadle rocks.

Soft as starlight or a dunter's down,
how the stole floats round your shoulders,
wool become wing, moorland made air,

as white as a tammie norie's breast,
as rock-cress clinging to the Keen.
Listen: you can hear the moon singing.

Enter the pattern, diamonds in diamonds,
chamfered waves. Watch them fall
round Humla Stack, the Holm of Skaw.

Love leads the weave, the lilting hours,
a woman sitting, haar at her door,
the dark at her back, mist in her fingers.

Stitch by stitch: a flick of her thumb.
Loop by loop the white poems come.

dunter – eider
Keen – Keen of Hamar
tammie norie – puffin

37

Owen Gallagher

Reading Braille in the Ark

In this room tongues dart over skin
deciphering messages as if reading Braille.
Fingers probe, stalk through brambles
the molecular structure in our bodies

temporarily astray. Here, language has no grip,
it is left outside, grappling on the mat,
signalling a truce, an amnesty,
whilst we place hope in ourselves, an ark,

fashioned from skin and bone and listen
to the waters rise, without star or oar,
not knowing where or when we might land,
perhaps at the feet of Noah.

David Betteridge

A Pierced Shell

Broken, rounded, smoothed: a sea-shell
sculpted by a long time's riddling waves.
Its centre shows a twist and fold,
where once a fluted column
and its maker-mollusc's living chamber
coiled. Necklace it;
or wear it on your pinkie as a ring;
or, through its hollow, view this shifting beach,
this sea, this everything.

The Journey Back

... how could I come
To what I am but by that deafening road,
Life-wide, world-wide, by which all come... ?
Edwin Muir

Go to any river that you know.
Trace it back to furthest, finest trickle of a source.
Ahead, above: the curving sky. Behind, below:
each uphill step you took against the river's course.
With your hand – perhaps – you could divert the stream;
or, with a wish, translate it: trickle,
shall we say, to Danube? – Jordan? – Indus? – anywhere...
Seeing it, and having travelled it,
you know the changes of direction
it would need. The same is true of words.
Choose one. Trace it back
and back and back, through times and tongues,
through different usages by different folk.
This journey of your mind
will lead you roundabout by ancient tracks
to where you are; and let you see
anew what truths remain,
and how each twist and turn of speech
helps the course of thought run wise.

Mark Leech

Dorsal

Your bones can feel so small
when I hold your back they gather,
gems in the panniers of my hands

shimmering streamwards through the weave
a bright arc, your back eases
graces as if a tailfin flashed

over the shallow bed
smoothed by palms of water, your back
in morning a fresh beach

stretching level into breezes,
your back a welcome landfall
for the soles of my hands

Isobel Lusted

Black Boat – March 2003

I was up early, dawn
really, mist on the marsh,
the Brede sliding dark past the window
when she came abreast slipping out
on the ebb, her black hull
laced with the beginnings of light,
a cowled figure dark as her skin
riding astern hand on tiller.

Out there you were waiting
on the border: Kuwait is all sand
and beetles you wrote, and
thanked me for your eighteenth
birthday gift. I could not think
of a poem as others were doing,
I could think only of prayer.

Martin Dodsworth

Landscapes and Traditions

Roy Fisher, *The Long and the Short of It: Poems 1955–2005*, Bloodaxe, £12.00

John Kinsella, *Peripheral Light: New and Selected Poems*, selected and with an introduction by Harold Bloom, Norton, £9.99; *The New Arcadia: Poems*, Norton, £14.99

Alan Jenkins, *A Shorter Life*, Chatto, £9.00

David Harsent, *Legion*, Faber, £8.99

John Stammers, *Stolen Love Behaviour*, Picador, £8.99

W.D. Jackson, *From Now to Then*, Menard Press/ School of Humanities, King's College, London, £9.99

Samuel Menashe, *New and Selected Poems*, Library of America, $20.00

The Long and the Short of It does not give us every poem that Roy Fisher has ever written, but it comes as close to that as he is prepared to go; it makes a substantial book, and one that should be on every bookshelf where there is an interest in poetry. Fisher is a modernist poet and, something rare in Britain, is a successful modernist poet. In the early days he was published by Cid Corman and Gael Turnbull, and for a while he lectured in American studies. But he feels like an English poet, not an imitator of the Americans. His Englishness in fact shows how well he has studied his American masters, translating their principled localism into a poetry of the English Midlands – not just the urban landscape of Birmingham where he grew up, but also the exploited hillsides of Derbyshire and Staffordshire. One of the best sections in this big book brings together his poems about poets. The Americans and their imitators are there, starting with Jonathan Williams as well as William Carlos, and going on to Lee Harwood and R.F. Langley, but so too are the British localists: Edwin Morgan, Jeremy Hooker and even Geoffrey Hill, who is a sort of localist in *Mercian Hymns*. You can't help being struck by the breadth of taste as well as by the way that taste is focused on artists each one of whom is in fruitful dialogue with Fisher himself.

That is one reason why a good place to start on Roy Fisher is with these poems which, whilst they are about or for other people, manage to say a good deal about Fisher himself. His tribute to Michael Hamburger is a case in point. On the surface they don't seem to have a lot in common, except that both are exceptionally gifted poets who haven't had their due in terms of readership. Fisher's way in is devious; his poem is called

'Style', and that's, in a way, what it turns out to be about. At first it looks as though Hamburger, an outstanding translator of many German poets, as well as a fine poet himself, is being sidelined, though he might be taken to know a bit about style too. 'Style?' says Fisher, 'I couldn't begin', and so begins. It's elegant, it's teasing, and it's poetic all at once, as he characterizes style as

> That marriage (like a supple glove
> that won't suffer me to breathe)
> to the language of one's time
> and class. The languages
> of my times and classes.

Fisher doesn't want to be pinned down in the way English people do pin you down as they sum up your accent and your dress; his poetry tries to get free of all that, and the ease with which these wry lines take you into his confidence is a mark of how he succeeds.

> I'd rather reach the air
> as a version by my friend Michael.
> He knows good Englishes.
> And he knows the language
> language gets my poems out of.

There's marriage and there's friendship; there's English and there's English. Language and language. In this poem, as in so many others, Fisher seems to see beyond language, which is at once a quarry for poetry and a prison-house (or a supple glove) poetry can escape – as here. The studied neutrality of 'Style' is unmarked by the language of Fisher's own class and time, and yet it is unmistakably *his* poem, one in which he can breathe, just as it is also Hamburger's, who knows – no hedging there – the language it comes out of, or is in, the language poets breathe.

Fisher's art is so subtle that there is something cruel about hanging over it in this way. He excels in lightness of touch, a principled lightness that resists type-casting. At the end of 'Style' there is something of the Cheshire Cat as the poet deftly removes himself from view. He insists the poems aren't about himself, not just implicitly in this poem, but, at the end of his acknowledgments, in so many words:

> These poems no more amount to a biography than I do; and my
> habits of working on projects from time to time over long periods
> and my heterodox approach to the methods I use would make an

arrangement that seemed chronologically false: so nothing of the kind
is here attempted.

I think that any one would smell a rat here. He does, after all, date every
poem (but only in the index of titles and first lines), and he has written
a very informative 'Antebiography' as well as taking part in interviews
which deal with his private life as well as his art (they are collected in
a valuable book called *Interviews Through Time*). The nine sections of
The Long and the Short of It are not so coherent as to tell you more than
a chronological arrangement, however approximate, would.

Distinctive as the sensibility is, though, and rooted in a particular series
of life-events, you will not necessarily feel the need to pin Fisher down.
However much he works his own experience of life, the fact that it is
his is rarely of prime importance. This is a poetry which is largely about
the existence of the world out there before the self. Writing about himself,
he has said: 'He doesn't judge his material; he lets it judge him, in the
form of his ability to perceive and render it. If he can't see anything he
can't say anything.' Many of the poems are little epiphanies, in which
the recipient barely figures, or if he does appear it is to be discounted in
one way or another. Take the opening of a relatively recent poem, 'Item':

A bookend. Consider it well
if that's the way your mind
runs. One-handed

this year at least, and lame,
unable to shift it somewhere better
than where it unbalances

one of the unsafe heaps that
make up my workroom, even I
get driven to consider it,

putting myself at risk of unaccustomed
irony, metaphor, moral.
It's one of a couple...

The poet is here all right, but he shifts the responsibility onto the bookend
– it's *driven* him to look at it. A few crumbs of personalia are granted
us – his lameness, the one-handed-ness, which are the product of his
stroke – but the suggestion of 'irony, metaphor, moral' take us away from
any further insight into his workroom and his way of life there. From

now on the poem is about the bookend, 'softwood,// deep-stained as oak and varnished/ heavily'. Its physical presence bulks large. It is like the trolleybus at the beginning of *A Furnace*:

November light low and strong
crossing from the left
finds this archaic
trolleybus, touches the side of it up
into solid yellow and green.

This is the country of the red wheelbarrow, but one where history is more acutely felt, the archaic emerging into the light. The bookend similarly embodies a past which the poet uncovers. Current practice would term it a 'transgressive' past; the bookend was made 'using materials, tools and time stolen/ from the Ministry of Aircraft Production', and its making is associated by the poet with 'Another little knot of illegalities', a backyard war-time abortion. Fisher is anarchist by inclination, and he is interested in transgression, but it is the way he stands back from the poem and allows it to judge him, as he once more disappears at the end of the poem, that seems to me most striking and typical. 'As to this bookend, to say that the first/ load it supported was a set of crimson-backed miniature/ home encyclopaedias.../ would be artistic, ironic, and, just possibly, untrue.' It would be artistically ironic because Beaverbrook who pushed the encyclopaedias was later Minister of Aircraft Production. If it were untrue, that would be perhaps because the man who made the bookcase felt the weight of his daughter's abortion as he made it. But the poet, who knows everything in the poem, doesn't know that. The past is not entirely recoverable and the self is not entirely knowable.

Fisher's poems are more about presenting states of mind than anything else. His working-class upbringing is important to him and to many of his readers, and it is the basis of what he sees in many of his poems. The poems, however, set out to take us to places in the mind that we haven't necessarily visited before. Surrealism is important to him, and modernist painting: *representation* is often not the point. An excellent poem, 'The Home Pianist's Companion', starting out from his own practice as a jazz pianist, superimposes the visual – railway wagon wheels, the 'mask of a narrow-faced cat', the 'vestigial' figure of an elderly neighbour remembered from earliest childhood – on the audible 'fifths/ and fourths in both hands', as the feel of playing is conjured up. Its object is to *present* this 'disorder of twofold sense', but also to go further than that, to what the 'gaunt, narrow-faced, closed-in' neighbour reminds him of:

what it was like to be sure,
before language ever
taught me they were different,
of how some things were the same.

The doubleness leads to a sameness, one that predates language and is
beyond it, and though the sameness obviously has something to do with
the limitations of the life that neighbour led (or suffered), it also connects
with the deep language underlying language in 'Style'. Fisher is a stout
Gibbonian rationalist by his own account, but the poetry is fascinated by
what the language of rationalism cannot capture. It is haunted by a kind
of post-Christian metaphysic; and it is haunting. That is one good reason
why *The Long and the Short of It* should be on your bookshelf. If you
haven't read him before, however, I'd caution you against the collection
of essays about him, *The Thing about Roy Fisher*, which John Kerrigan
and Peter Robinson edited a few years back. It has its uses, of course,
but there is too much exposition of ideas, too little comment on the way
the poems feel. Fisher's ambitious long poem *A Furnace* is handled a bit
uncritically; it is interesting but not as varied as it needs to be. The
structure is not helpful and expressive in the way Fisher wants it to be,
and that, I think, is because he is a poet of epiphanies rather than the
long run. Although he sometimes seems to feel that his earliest 'big'
work, the poem *City*, was mangled in the process of being edited, Michael
Shayer was probably right to cut and paste what is, and remains, even
after the author's further revision, a sort of urban collage. Glimpses,
intimations, uncertainties are what Fisher's poetry is about. His greatest
affinity among the Americans is probably with George Oppen.

Fisher's poetry is often tied to particular places, parts of Birmingham,
bits of Derbyshire. He goes as far afield as Brittany. But he has said that
'the "place" tag is not very meaningful' to him, that his subject matter
is more a matter of memory than topography. That is credible. With John
Kinsella, who writes largely, but far from exclusively, about his own part
of Western Australia, place seems to have greater importance. Ostensibly,
his poems are about ecology, the degradation of a landscape as the result
of human action. His own history appears only occasionally. Yet his
poetry does, after all, have something in common with Fisher's; perhaps
it is that he gives his own appearances in the poetry so little emphasis,
perhaps it is that he also seems to be challenged by the landscape he
depicts. In his suggestive introduction to *Peripheral Light*, a substantial
and well-chosen selection, Harold Bloom remarks that Kinsella's originality
is one of sensibility and temperament: 'He perceives and senses almost
occultly'. That is rather sybilline, but if it means that Kinsella himself is

rarely seen to be perceiving, whilst his poetry is full of perception, then it is itself perceptive. The poetry is haunted by the poet's absent presence. The landscapes are largely ruined landscapes, brilliantly registered, with little direct comment, but this restraint is felt as tension in the verse. Take the opening of a poem called 'Hectic Red': 'Quartz sparks randomly/ on the pink and white crust/ of the salt flats...' The unqualified statement is simple and direct, but also uncomfortable in the juxtaposition of sound in its first two words. And there is more discomfort to come; the sentence continues for another seventeen short lines before there is any pause, and even then its direction remains uncertain, everything, the whole poem, depending grammatically, but with elusive logic, from that sparking quartz which *says* nothing, like the sacks of grain, 'lips sewn shut,/ packed tight, flexing dust/ and dragging their feet'. It takes one back to Fisher and his material judging *him*. 'Hectic Red' in one aspect is all 'material' sitting in judgment on the artist and on his perceiving and rendering.

Kinsella is a prolific poet. There are about a hundred poems in his latest book, *The New Arcadia*. This prodigal creativity makes it difficult to focus on what is going on in his work; the eye is dazzled. He works through the same landscape again and again, so that one might wonder if one isn't just seduced by the exoticism of the wandoos, jam-trees, skinks and mallees and the thought of that primitive life of farmers killing their land under the harsh Australian sun. Undoubtedly this is part of the attraction, but there is also the poet's furious verbal energy to bring into the account – a small example might be that suggestive phrase 'flexing dust' describing the sacks of grain in 'Hectic Red'. The imagination is continually driving the language to innovate. This force is exciting and disturbing; it derives from an unseen source. 'I never write "confessional" poetry,' he says, but the tension in the verse seems to spring from unvoiced confession. Matters are further complicated by Kinsella's engagement with postmodernity. Neither of the books here is 'experimental' in the way of his *Doppler Effect*, but he does, like J.H. Prynne, use the language of technology, does resist the commodification of poetry by a less than winning violence to rhythm and syntax, and does his best to render a de-centred self. It all adds up to this, that reading Kinsella is an exciting, invigorating, often uncomfortable and challenging experience. Both the books here reviewed should be required reading for anyone who takes contemporary poetry seriously, even if *The New Arcadia* does not quite fulfil the expectations (of epic scope, of encounter with the historic past of Philip Sidney) to which it gives rise. There are, for all that, some wonderful poems there – and Kinsella's genius is not one that manifests itself in polish and coherence, but in fascinated submission and tormented outburst. You have to think in terms of Lord Byron's 'lava of the imagination whose eruption prevents an earthquake'.

It is possible that Alan Jenkins would also wish to be thought of in these terms, though Baudelaire and Rimbaud figure more largely in his imagining. The poems in *A Shorter Life* take us back to (less of) the punishing sex-and-naughtiness, as well as (more of) the commemoration of dead friends and of his parents, that have characterized his four previous volumes. There seems little point in complaining that Jenkins doesn't 'develop'; what he does he does very well. That very acute and downright critic Kenneth Cox crowned him with bays: 'The apparition of a poet with the force and range of Alan Jenkins calls for more than cursory notice' (*Agenda*, 37.1). I think one must demur at 'range', but the force is certainly here in this new book – the force of language, which Cox noted ('taboo words inserted without a second thought') and a force of impossible desire, as in 'As If', a poem in memory of Kathy Acker. Turning off US 101 in his car the poet gets out and starts clawing at the earth

> as if, as if
> I might open wide its great cunt and it give birth,
> as if I might get down to what was left,
> the tattoos on her arms and back,
> the scars of her breasts, the sour-sweet whiff
> of her arse...

The poet's intention hardly seems to be to make a well-mannered, well-wrought urn. The lava is in full flow. Yet this poem rhymes very completely and its three stanzas reflect each other in artful symmetry. The disorder of experience and the extravagance of feeling are not 'contained' (the poem is one long sentence driving *through* the stanza-breaks), but coexist beside a shadowy, shadowing idea of order, which offers its own unhappy commentary on them. There is something very English about this. Larkin didn't stage the famous photograph of himself sitting by the 'England' road-sign simply in order to depict himself as a fuddy-duddy patriot, but also to link his peculiar brand of frustrated passion and yearning for simplicity with the culture (middle-class, repressed, self-protective) that was his. Witness 'To the Sea', but there are plenty of other possible examples. Jenkins shares that culture, and the moving poems about his mother in *A Shorter Life* bear comparison with things like 'Love Songs in Age'. They are moving because in them simplicity is achieved by indirection and too late, but is achieved. In 'Launderette: Her Last Nightdress' the nightdress that pleased his mother as she neared her death in hospital, 'A cotton one with a few flowers and a bit of lace', becomes the means for Jenkins to express the otherwise inexpressible. Stained by her illness it tumbles out among the machines with his 'socks and shirts and smalls',

> A stench I took away with me somehow
> To wash, and forgot about till now
> I stand here in the warm soap-smelling air

> But can't remember why, and people stare.

The placing of the last line is pure Larkin, but it doesn't matter, because Jenkins so thoroughly understands the place from which he writes. Kenneth Cox, used largely to the modern American tradition, failed to see the Englishness in Jenkins's verse but had such fine sensibility that he couldn't but respond to it.

A *Shorter Life* made it to the short list for the Forward Prize for 2005, but the prize was given to David Harsent for *Legion*. The title-sequence is about war and the devils it unleashes; it pulls no punches:

> They told us about the boy who disappeared
> when the convoy went through. Search
> as they might there was no sign until word
> was sent of 'residue' between the wheel and the wheel-arch.

The half-rhymes, the enjambment, the oblique third-person plural and the euphemistic 'residue' all make their point directly and without fuss. There is much that is admirable about this writing. It seems indecent to complain that no one who reads Harsent is likely to be under any illusions about the nature of war. But it has to be said. There is something too well-managed about the way these poems are realized. The word 'residue' might well figure in a written Army report, but not in speech. The word holds at a distance not only the boy's death but also the feelings about it of 'them' – that is what it is for. It doesn't mean that 'they' don't have feelings, and it is a limitation of these poems that their sympathies don't extend to imagining those feelings. Harsent's writing is in many ways brilliant, for example, in the way he rhymes with punishing inventiveness on almost a single rhyme through a whole poem, but the right to punish the reader in this fashion is not unequivocally established. That is why, had I been a Forward judge I should have inclined to the more psychologically complex Jenkins.

A *Shorter Life* includes two elegies for the critic (and poet) Ian Hamilton, who published early poems by Harsent in *the review*. He was another representative of the repressed English tradition, sardonic, self-lacerating, only loosening up under the influence of nicotine and alcohol. Harsent stands for the side of Hamilton that rode headlong to judgment (his *Poetry Chronicle*, harsh, comic and often unjust, reflects a desolating fear of emotion). Jenkins answers to the tight-lipped admissions of feeling in Hamilton's poems with something franker and brave, if just as unhappy.

Short shrift, I'm afraid, for my remaining three books, of which the first two well deserve reading – the third requires it. John Stammers writes about the search for love in wonderfully unaffected and perceptive language, as in a short poem where lovers talk in a deserted autumnal car park 'like double agents.../ you telling me to me, me telling you to you.' *Stolen Love Behaviour* is slight and not rich in self-knowledge, but is also a perfectly focused expression of what it is to be young, unattached and male in sort-of-literary London. *From Now to Then* has less of perfection. It is conceived as the second volume of three, reflecting on time and memory. W.D. Jackson has lived in Germany since 1973 and the reason you should read this book is that it contains convincingly powerful versions of many poems by Heine, as well as a long passage from Lessing's *Nathan the Wise*. The reflections on time and memory set them within a complicated autobiographical structure, allusive and perhaps evasive, which does not quite justify itself. It is a volume in which to pick and choose. Finally, Samuel Menashe is an American poet who specializes in extremely brief but memorable poems ('Beachhead', for example: 'The tide ebbs/ from a helmet/ wet sand embeds') and has always had greater success in Britain than in his own country (Donald Davie was an early admirer). His *New and Selected Poems* really does offer the best of his work, and there is an excellent introduction by Christopher Ricks. Congratulations also to the Library of America for elegant design.

William Bedford

Crediting Poetry

Seamus Heaney's *District and Circle*, Faber 2006, £12.99 hardback

In his 1995 Nobel Lecture 'Crediting Poetry',[1] Heaney made a characteristic leap from a childhood memory – 'we were as susceptible and impressionable as the drinking water that stood in a bucket in our scullery: every time a passing train made the earth shake, the surface of that water used to ripple delicately, concentrically, and in utter silence'[2] – to an adult recognition of the power of poetry – 'I credit it … because poetry can make an order as true to the impact of external reality and as sensitive to the inner laws of the poet's being as the ripples that rippled in and rippled out across the water in that scullery bucket fifty years ago'.[3] Such ordering was always implicit in the poems – one might almost say in the nature of poetry – but it becomes explicit in even the titles with *Seeing Things* (1991), *The Spirit Level* (1996) and *Electric Light* (2001). 'I began a few years ago to try to make space in my reckoning and imagination for the marvellous as well as for the murderous',[4] the poet explained in his Nobel Lecture, and *District and Circle* is another stage on this powerful, illuminating journey.

The 'murderous' seems to be explicit and contemporary in 'District and Circle' (pp.17–19) with its journey into the underworld of the London Underground, 'Helmet' (p. 14) with its reference to a 'Boston fireman's' helmet, and the apparent concern with global warming in the melting glacier in 'Höfn' (p. 53). Reviewers have already wondered aloud whether 'District and Circle' and 'Helmet' were written before or after the London and New York bombings, but this seems to me irrelevant. The resonances are there, but it is the nature of Heaney's achievement that they are *always* there. And they go deeper than contemporary history. 'District' is a very Heaney word, that sense of place which was the theme of one of the longest essays in *Preoccupations*,[5] and 'Circle' reminded me immediately of the very first sentence in that collection with its repeated '*omphalos, omphalos, omphalos*' that 'marked the centre of the world'.[6] This journey underground is a journey with Dante and Orpheus, and the Boston fireman's helmet is both a gift from twenty years ago and an image from the New York atrocity.

Childhood is permeated by rumours of war. In 'Polish Sleepers' (p. 6) the child Heaney hears the goods trains from Castledawson at night, but the sleepers they cross are Polish, and what the adult poet hears in 'Each

51

languid, clanking waggon' is implied in that single word, 'Polish', and then the chilling 'And afterwards, *rust, thistles, silence, sky.*' 'Anahorish 1944' (p. 7) brings with it an entire history in the title's date and an opening line, 'We were killing pigs when the Americans arrived,' and 'To Mick Joyce in Heaven" (pp. 8–10) and 'The Aerodrome' (pp. 11–12) focus the attention in the same way, and then make the telling point:

> If self is a location, so is love:
> Bearings taken, markings, cardinal points,
> Options, obstinacies, dug heels and distance,
> Here and there and now and then, a stance (p. 12).

This is most finely achieved in 'The Nod' (p. 33) where a childhood memory of Saturday evenings in 'Loudan's butcher shop' with all its 'seeping blood' prompts another memory of 'the local B-Men' nodding at the poet's father 'As if deliberately they'd aimed and missed him.' History is always with us in these poems, in Heaney's intense meditation under pressure. And it is history which goes a long way back. 'Anything Can Happen' (p. 13) is 'after Horace' with Jupiter hurling 'the lightning' and 'the clogged underearth' bringing another ghost to 'District and Circle', and 'Out of Shot' (p. 15) has a November morning in Wicklow, but with the 'Viking *vik*' and 'Norse raids, night-dreads' to remind us of another nightmare.

And then there are the deeper, the more personal resonances, the spirit level if you like, the imagist, the epiphanic: 'the reel' of metal runners 'on frozen Windermere' in 'Wordsworth's Skates' (p. 22); and 'Dorothy young, jig-jigging her iron shovel', and 'Dorothy old … all the companions/Gone or let go, their footfalls on the road/Unlistened for, that sounded once as plump/As the dropping shut of the flap-board scuttle-lid/The minute she'd stacked the grate for their arrival' in 'Home Fires' (p. 70): all these marvellous moments 'like well water far down' in 'Out of This World' (p. 47). Some of these moments come in autobiographical and prose poems of great power, such as 'One Christmas Day in the Morning' (p. 31) and three wonderful sequences in 'Found Prose' (pp. 36–41), but for me Heaney's characteristic achievement is most movingly seen in 'Edward Thomas on the Lagans Road' (p. 35). In this wonderful poem, the ghost of Edward Thomas disturbs lovers in their lovemaking, so that 'they rise and go' and the poet is left alone:

> And now the road is empty.
> Nothing but air and light between their love-nest
> And the bracken hillside where I lie alone.

Utter evening, as it was in the beginning,

Until the remembered come and go of lovers
Brings on his long-legged self on the Lagans Road –
Edward Thomas in his khaki tunic
Like one of the Evans brothers out of Leitrim,
Demobbed, 'not much changed', sandy moustached
    and freckled
From being, they said, with Monty in the desert.

An entire people's history moves in this poem, indeed two people's history, the Great War and the Troubles entering our national psyches like a wound, a great poet saluting another great poet across a history that is 'about as instructive as an abattoir'.[7] What Heaney hopes for in 'Crediting Poetry' he achieves here and in so many other poems.

    I have two favourites in *District and Circle*, poems that take us back to Heaney's own beginnings as a writer, and therefore I suppose for some of us our own beginnings as readers. 'Quitting Time' (p. 69) returns to the water pump in the farmyard Heaney has written about so often, and his father finishing work at the end of the day, saying a sort of farewell. 'More and more this last look at the wet/Shine of the place is what means most to him', the repeated phrase 'My head is light' resting between so many meanings, and then the closing of the gate, 'The song of a tubular steel gate in the dark/As he pulls it to and starts his uphill trek.' The final poem in the collection, 'The Blackbird of Glanmore' (pp. 75–6) returns to Glanmore, the scene of some of Heaney's greatest sonnets, and now he is welcomed by a familiar blackbird, and thinks of his father, and of the death of the brother he wrote about so movingly and so long ago in the poem 'Mid-Term Break' in *Death of a Naturalist*, and his long 'house of life'. Yet the blackbird is there 'On the grass when I arrive/In the ivy when I leave', an image which says it all.

    What I feel as I read and begin to own *District and Circle* is a sense of gratitude. After all the theoretical talk of the marvellous and the murderous, one's mind begins to settle, the 'quicksand of relativism'[8] fades, and one is left with the poems, with the actual, with the real, as the older poets and philosophers would have said, as Heaney himself might say. This is a wonderful collection, by a wonderful poet.

[1] 'Crediting Poetry,' *Opened Ground* (Faber,1998).   [2] Ibid, p. 447.
[3] Ibid, pp. 449–50.   [4] Ibid, p. 458.
[5] 'The Sense of Place', *Preoccupations* (Faber, 1980).   [6] Ibid, p. 17.
[7] *Opened Ground*, p. 456.   [8] Ibid, p. 453.

Michael Kinsella

Chosen Young Broadsheet essayist, 36, lives in Northern Ireland. He is a freelance writer and reviewer and is currently writing a piece on crushes.

The Precariousness of Privacy

Seamus Heaney, *District and Circle*, Faber, 2006, £12.99 hardback

'Private', Raymond Williams wrote, 'is still a complex word'. It refers to a withdrawal from public life and is used to legitimize place and protect personal space. Synonymous with privilege, it is often used to conceal how the intimate life gets lived. In a sense, it is everything associated with home and the very things we are least at home with. And it is private life – in its literal and abstract sense – which is the focus of many of the poems in *District and Circle*.

In the last poem in the book, 'The Blackbird of Glanmore', Heaney visits his cottage retreat in Co.Wicklow. If it is, as the poet says, 'his house of life' – since *Field Work* (1979) Glanmore has come to represent his commitment to writing and the solitude of a literary life – it is there he has the privilege of being able to breathe in stillness. But this is a poem that also locates itself in elsewheres. It goes back to 'The Wood', Heaney's second boyhood home, to the death of his brother Christopher, and the terrible homesickness Heaney felt when he spent his first term as a boarder at St Columb's College, Derry. These references bring to mind the early poems, 'Mid-Term Break' (*Death of a Naturalist*, 1966) and 'The Ministry of Fear' (*North*, 1975) evoking some of the most intense feelings of loss and anger in Heaney's oeuvre when what was deeply felt would generate a terrific flurry of creativity. If these early autobiographical poems represent a life where the private and the privacy to write went hand in hand, 'The Blackbird of Glanmore' does not seem to parade such confidence. Although Heaney has described the poem as his favourite in the collection, this is not a piece where the Nobel Laureate struts his stuff, but a poem of diminished confidence and therefore more interesting because diminished.

Altogether 'nervy', Heaney seems lacking in confidence about receiving inspiration. He sees in the blackbird's 'panic ... a bird's eye view of myself', as the locking of the car's doors threatens to scare off the creature. Unlike his early collections, there are no insistent signals here. And should we think of the blackbird as symbolic of the poet's ability to sing, then the car's locks could be said to represent the wider world, a digital age of cash machines, scanners and transatlantic flights – one which the poet readies himself for in *District and Circle*, just like the spirit of the preserved bog-body in 'The Tollund Man in Springtime'. As with *Electric Light* (2001), Heaney continues to incorporate the language of modern technology into his poetry – or perhaps the locking car doors could hint to Heaney's other life as ambassador of poetry and how, in doing the decent thing, his duties have been a form of self-sabotage and 'wrong moves'. Yet, despite this intrusive element, Glanmore, as his place of writing, through the privacies it gives the poet and the private moments it invites, with each return and departure of inspiration, Heaney is determined to steel himself for the future: 'I am absolute/ For you, your ready talkback,/ Your each stand-offish comeback,/ Your picky, nervy goldbeak – / On the grass when I arrive, // In the ivy when I leave.' And the jitteriness of these lines, the not-quite-sureness, the risk and reach for the next moment – as in the depressed Wordsworthian vision in 'On the Spot', where Heaney recalls the 'stigma' of finding rotten eggs – serve to make this collection vital, edgy, urgent.

The poet's private home at Glanmore is once again the subject of intrusions upon the private life in 'Polish Sleepers'. What could potentially be a pastoral scene – pastoral being a kind of decadent privacy – gets disrupted when the poet imagines 'tarry pus … bearing forward to the garden' oozing from railway sleepers. And once again memories from childhood come shunting through the poem, turning a goods train into a vehicle for mass extermination. Like 'The Blackbird of Glanmore' and 'Polish Sleepers', 'The Birch Grove' seems to want us to wonder – when we are at home, what are we at home with? The idyllic scene – breezy, white, cool, musical – gives us all the privileges of private life. But the walled garden acts as a fairly solid reminder that the private life is defined by what lies outside it. You can, the poem seems to suggest, be in private company. (As paradoxical as it might seem, you cannot be private by yourself.) And as the couple drink tea and quote from Joseph Brodsky: ' "If art teaches us anything,' he says, trumping life/ With a quote, "it's that the human condition is private" ' – Heaney notes that 'above them a jet trail/ Tapers and waves like a willow wand'. And that jet trail across what we imagine to be a blue sky is a subtle reminder of September 11 and how the private life is lived precariously.

To pun on the title from another poem in the collection, 'The Birch Grove' might well be a reminder that 'anything can happen'. And 'Anything Can Happen', a version of Horace's *Ode* I, 34, unlike the more oblique reference in 'The Birch Grove', was written in direct response to the attacks in America. It registers the shock of an individual, and how, out of the blue, the private life gets violated and belittled by the seemingly apocalyptic. 'Nothing resettles right', the panicked speaker says, 'Telluric ash and fire-spores boil away.' The poem reads like a kind of panicked confession, where personal safety and world security are left hopelessly overturned. In contrast, the collection's title poem, 'District and Circle', does not make explicit reference to the July 7 tube attacks, yet the private moment of the poem – the poet tells of a Dantesque descent into and journey through the underground while remaining faithful to that workaday experience – cannot simply be caught up in the energies and thrills of being 'transported/ Through galleried earth' or the awkward invasions of privacy when the poet's eyes meet that of a busker. Shut in with the poem's desire to be a personal recollection – it does not want to give history 'the last word', as the poet says elsewhere ('The Tollund Man in Springtime') – is a sympathy for those who suffered. It is couched in the language of grief. The concluding lines, which seem to be carried over from 'A Sofa in the Forties' (*The Spirit Level*, 1996) – a poem about child's play and the Holocaust – are reused, not in the service of 'making engine noise', as the children imitate the sounds of a train, but to highlight the cruel and brutal. The poet is 'hurtled forward' whilst looking at his reflection in a window, 'mirror-backed/ By blasted weeping rock-walls'.

Of all of Heaney's collections, *District and Circle* is perhaps the most knowingly self-referential. His earlier poetry gets worked into many of these poems. At times, some of them feel like fallen leaves from previous collections. 'Quitting Time' is one example. An intimate poem, of lowliness and loneliness that could be partnered with 'Keeping Going' (*The Spirit Level*, 1996). Another instance could be 'Moyulla', which seems to come harping from the same riverbed as 'Gifts of Rain' (*Wintering Out*, 1972). Then there are the 'bell' poems. 'Poet to Blacksmith' and 'Midnight Anvil' chime with 'The Forge' and 'Digging'. Other poems put on show things which Heaney's work has traditionally kept private. It is a surprise to encounter Miss Walls again, no longer the sweet teacher in 'Death of a Naturalist', but a more punishing figure who 'Lost her head and cut the legs off us/ For dirty talk', or to hear about Heaney's loss of faith, something he says, which 'occurred off-stage' (see 'Like everybody else...'), a private rejection perhaps in favour of the secular. Certainly, many of these poems could be described as supplementary to his previous work. They could even be seen as attempts to shape how his earlier work should be read and interpreted in the light of his schooling and Catholicism. Either way, to be so knowingly self-referential suggests that this collection should be thought of as something more than transitional. It could be described as a collection of guidings and testings, of directions taken and to take, little peeks of what has yet to come.

Myra Schneider

Playing with Fire

Grevel Lindop, *Playing With Fire*, Carcanet £9.95

Grevel Lindop has found a new and strongly personal voice in *Playing With Fire*. There is still the remarkable use of detail, thoughtful exploration of ideas, clarity and graceful ease with form but the distancing characteristic of most of his earlier work has gone. It is as if he has emerged from a cocoon.

An image of fire drives the opening poem which begins by focusing on logs in a basket and then shifts through contemporary news items, through history and geography to a powerful image of a forest: 'The green crowns drink sunlight until their dumb/hearts are glutted with fire' and this is transmuted to an image of creativity. The fire reference of the title links the book's four parts but its underlying theme is time. In the ambitious 'How Long Is the Coast of Britain?' Lindop explores geographical distance and time distance by coinciding memories about his children and his own childhood in different coastal areas. 'The Mirror', essentially a love poem, is framed round the idea of time and timelessness. It opens: 'I can even date it . . . the necklace we make to hang/ . . . round the lovely neck of the infinite and eternal'. 'Night' is a lyrical expression of the idea that 'Time is for the day' and 'night is timeless . . .' Time and memory underlie many other poems, the tender 'That Month' for example, about a vasectomy. 'A Dog at the Threshold' is a meditation, set off by looking at the dog resting on the lino, in which the poet considers the point he's reached in life with 'the three-headed dog of past, present, future' bristling 'beside me.'

Love is the key to this book: sexual love, romantic love, love in marriage and the idealization of love which is presented in dream and in images of a female deity. 'A Dozen Red Roses', written to the poet's wife, is a tour de force produced from a clichéd image. My favourite of these beautiful poems is: 'The Mirror' in which Lindop imagines himself after death when King Yama holds up a mirror and what shines within it:

> . . . will be a white waterfall
> and I a salmon who leaps it,
> will be the moon and the sun
> locked in their mutual eclipse;
> and the fire of their interlocking
> is what burns me now, love, and you.

The third section set in a striptease club is a trip into a palace of dreams and has analogies with poetry. I'm not fully convinced by these nor by the conversation with the dancers and though I like the poet's honesty, I find the descriptions of stripping and dancing repetitious and exploitative and the total picture, in spite of good observation, one-sided. The self-questioning engaged me but I wanted it to travel somewhere. For me these poems sat uncomfortably next to the others in this book.

The last section is a series of outstanding poems which investigate death in different ways. 'Genus Locii' looks at the transience of individual life and of the life of the planet. I read it as a credo and I find its vision and sense of acceptance extraordinarily reassuring and uplifting:

Nothing could be kept, of course: it was all evanescent
as the apricot-lace buttress of bunched and dissolving cloud
spilling now behind oakwood and white-rendered
barn... None of it was either
physical or mental, it was all both and beyond both...

Playing With Fire with its musicality, energy, intensity, spirituality and depth of thought is an achievement which marks Grevel Lindop as a serious poet. I strongly recommend this book.

Anita Money

Avril Bruten 05.04.40 – 19.01.06: A Commemoration

Poems, printed by Subscription, Oxford 1989
In the 'lost & found' columns, Oversteps Books, 2005. ISBN 0–9541376–8-X

Avril Bruten was a scholar, teacher and poet. She was also a Catholic. The medieval world so familiar to her in her studies, a time when England was culturally part of a Catholic Europe, becomes a natural extension of her contemporary world. The miniatures, symbols, biblical scenes, saints and liturgical calendar (she has poems on Lent, Ascension, Pentecost, Good Friday, On the Feast of the Annunciation) are shared imaginative resources for a very human understanding of life through a faith in life after death. There is no stridency here, no 'born again' zeal to deter even the believer but a personal searching, losing and finding.

There are recollections of journeys to a Mediterranean alive with Classical and Christian history (Garden of the Fugitives, Pompeii; Venice; Piazza Pitagora; S. Maria di Castellabate; Agrigento; St Catherine's Monastery in Sinai) and journeys of the mind to childhood, London and other places. The journey back from a loved place (S. Maria di Castellabate) conjures comparisons with swifts:

> 'East West
> Home's best.'
> But is it?
> I have watched the swifts ready,
> Steady, go ...
>
> We have a wider mouth to sing
> Than such a bird,
> More to say for ourselves.
> And yet, ...
>
> Here's our massive, our unlikely plane,
> Ready on the run
> Away, alert like swifts to an air-flow.
> Not a bit like us, though.
> A bit's always missing,
> We find. But have lost the scent of its traces.

There are 'In Memoriams' to friends (many from Oxford, home to

59

Avril Bruten from 1963 when she was appointed Tutorial Fellow in English Medieval Language and Literature at St Hugh's and a University lecturer, later becoming Fellow Emeritus of the College) and the coming to terms with sadness and loss through the seasons in the company of trees and plants in familiar gardens.

Her poems, none of which are long, have clarity, reticence and a particular speaking voice – natural, humorous and questioning, open to answers and instructive, colloquial where it suits:

What can the old life tell us?

Replies come up like elm roots
Far from the trunk breaking
The orderly asphalt.

Her technique is often playful, homophones and monosyllabic endings and internal rhyme used to a noticeable degree, syntax highlighted in the careful juxtaposing of even the smallest parts of speech to catch distinctions of sense. Little wonder that she, who has written on St Augustine's theory of the Art of Rhetoric, should use the twists and turns which lurk in language, pointers to so many views.

So many things left said
Stand in the air,
Like the sound of the saw in the head
When the dead elms are down
And the job is over.

Death, real as a man, strolls red
Or black, some say. Spare,
Some say. With a determined tread,
Some say. Some say, with a crown.
Or gross and over-

Fed, some say. But some are led
To quietness. There
Are, they think, these hints: ...
('Points of View')

In 'The Grayling in the Grieving' from her recent book, a contemplation of human death and separation opens to an awareness of other forms of life and another kind of voice:

We go our separate ways
As the dead and breathing always do.
Long and sudden, loss
Will race ahead and trudge
Behind us, nights and days,
Seconds, minutes, months and lifetimes cross
Our roads although we cannot budge
From dwelling upon, within, our tired habitual dwelling.

Loss pampers our failing
To see through this hinged pair
Of wings: a breath and its death
Upon the same track
And running no race
And cannot look back,
Nor ahead.
So what can we do?

You? Says a voice
In the jasmine. As its flowers fall,
Still the still probing
Tendrils tell us: *Nothing at all.*
What's the choice?
Nothing is up (nor is it down) to you.

Even the Grayling, too.
Gathers close its graceful wings by an other grace.

As plants, birds and butterflies have a strong and beneficial presence (see the ironic 'Eye Test' which plays on seeing and understanding), so also do emblematic animals like the Deer, Icthus, Hare and Pelican.

People have always been at a push
What to call it. This word, that word weaves
Through psalm and proverb, stabbing to name
It: rock-badger, coney, rock-rabbit, Old Tom
(says Surtees). And what it stands for, drifting
To madness and the uncloseable eye,
Through monkish margins, gem-bright
Witness to Christ's healing acts ...
('Hare')

Or from 'The Pelican':

Friend who has stood in the dark,
And has known the light swell back –
Its crumpled vision;
And knows the backward way,
Also – let me talk
In shadows for a time,
Re-learn to walk
Along the edge of them,
Feeling, though failing, to see
How they fit to the clock's day
And night.

Neither the falcon,
Angered, nor the silent swan,
But the one who has fed
Where its own breast bled,
Leads the lost on.

In her second book, dedicated to St Anthony of Padua, 'Patron of all who are trying to find what is lost', she used the persona of Joyce in 'Columns' to describe a sense of imaginative deflation and isolation on a package visit to Rome and the Coliseum with her husband Jack, whose 'Why roam?' becomes an ironic echo. In 'Lost and Found', she speaks in her own voice and, in the process of sorting out old papers to throw away pre the intention to retire – 'Chapel-cards, Birthday cards, cards for all/ For nothing days, once all-or-nothing days' – finds a note: ' "**Before the Proceedings Commence, / Li Li Sha will play SEA WAVES WASHING THE SAND."** '

What were those proceedings? Who was she?
Which was her instrument: keyboard? Strings?
Where the sea's waves washing which sand?
Nothing in present mind or memory rings
Recognition. Yet, I seem to care:
Li Li Sha. Li Li Sha, – now where?
Still playing before proceedings? Dead and
Dumb? Did I applaud you? Smiling, thank your hand?

If I was there?

The questions hang in the air, a dialogue with memory, time, understanding, and a vanished person. In an earlier poem, 'Song from the Off-shore', an interesting modulation of voice occurs: 'I think you should not think of going back', ending with:

> Yes, you will return – because the shell tells tales
> No more now to be believed than when it sang
> Of hope and slid a blade of magic, charm,
> Of expectation, through the heart; and the wind
> Got up angry, well out of dreadful reach
> Of the safe bay, crooked like a mother's arm.

If mortality is mirrored in miniature in 'In a moment I'll leave this moment's place' from 'On the Via Dolorosa', the Christian mystery of the Incarnation is given its human and odd reality in 'At Zachariah's House' where Mary, lonely and in need of friendship, visits Elizabeth. Both are pregnant and Mary already knows the future.

> And it was odd
> (No word's enough),
> You hugging me like a daughter
>
> And the mother of God.
> I am always that
> From start to end and after.
>
> I remember the future.

These thoughtful poems which have so light a touch, know well the irony of our evolved status, our silent sympathy with other living things serving as a respite from the precarious nature of language. 'Song of Degrees', which Avril Bruten always included in readings, introduces her first book and closes her second:

'I am for peace: but when I speak, they are for war' (Psalm 120)

> And it has never broken
> Through my iron skull
> That they might be for peace.
> Had I not spoken.

William Bedford

Of Diligence and Jeopardy

Geoffrey Hill, *Style and Faith*, Counterpoint, 2003, £8.70, £17.99 hardback

In his 'Preface,' Hill disavows any 'desire to add my voice to the chorus of contemporary cultural lament, a centrifugal movement in which immense generalizations are produced out of solipsistic rancour' (p. xiii). He remains insistently attentive to those sixteenth and seventeenth century writers already discussed in *The Lords of Limit* and *The Enemy's Country*, where the very language sounds remote from our dismayed concerns:

> I am prepared to argue ... that it is a characteristic of the best English writing of the early sixteenth to late seventeenth centuries that authors were prepared and able to imitate the original authorship, the *auctoritas*, of God, at least to the extent that forbade them to be idle spectators of their own writing (ibid).

And again:

> It strikes me that the sentences from Calvin with which I began could stand as an epigraph to John Donne's several presentations of an essential theme throughout his devotional writing: that of God's grammar. It is a question whether we now understand, let alone receive, this grammar as Donne intended us to grasp it:

> > The Holy Ghost is an eloquent Author, a vehement, and an abundant Author, but yet not luxuriant; he is far from a penurious, but as far from a superfluous style too.

> With Donne, style is faith: a measure of delivery that confesses his own inordinacy while remaining in all things ordinate (pp. xiii–xiv).

The language of religion and Deity seem to place the issues firmly in the sixteenth and seventeenth centuries, but philosophically the issue is to do with authority, as urgently though not fatally relevant today as it was for Hooker and Hobbes, Donne and Vaughan. Gödel's passionately Platonic geometry or George Steiner's *Real Presences* occupy the same territory. Listen to any contemporary politician and you are hearing a language which is straining against the pressure of authority as relentlessly as in the sixteenth and seventeenth centuries. It would be a self-serving error to assume that *Style and Faith* is not about ourselves. The fact that Hill also returns insistently to Hopkins and Eliot merely serves to clarify the point.

The first two essays deal with lexicography and Biblical translation. 'Common Weal, Common Woe' reviews the Second Edition of *The Oxford English Dictionary* (1989), discussing Murray's founding principles and the tensions between philology and Coleridge's 'activity of the assimilative and of the modifying faculties' (p. 19), and Empson's 'the interactions of the senses of a word' (p. 4). Coleridge, of course, was 'constitutionally against the "set"' (p. 15) of his time, his prose 'characterized by phrases descriptive of resisting the current' (ibid), and Empson's insistence was always upon the manner in which words 'straddle' (p. 5) logical distinctions in their 'going together' (ibid). This is not to question Murray's philological emphasis, but to wonder whether 'the very nobility of its achievement is inseparable from the stubbornness of its flaws' (p. 19). By 'flaws' Hill is referring, for example, to the OED's 'vigilance of such generous scope' (p. 2) in recording between 1884 and 1933 ten citations of the word *Disremember* but over that same half-century failing 'to recognise the one usage which significantly changes the pitch of the word' (pp. 2–3), Hopkins's 'qùite/Disremembering, dìsmèmbering àll now'. Hopkins's genius might be thought to raise inevitable problems for philology, his 'going together' and his coinages, such as *unchancelling*, which indeed remains 'off the record' (p. 19) as far as the OED is concerned. Hill is perfectly well aware of the choices involved here, but challenges the editors with his view that 'the genius of the language is peculiarly determined by, and is correlatively a determinant of, "the special endowments which fit a man for his peculiar work"' (pp. 14–15). The latter is Hobbes, with his strong views on '"exact definitions first snuffed, and purged from ambiguity"' (p. 15), and as always Hill writes brilliantly about those sixteenth and seventeenth century writers 'whose stylistic strengths sprang mainly from the need to make radical distinctions and to prescribe the limits of signification' (p. 7), for example Clarendon's use of *dexterity* in *History of the Rebellion* (p. 5), and Hobbes's *undiscerned, undiscerning* (p. 12), a crucial discrimination ignored by the original OED reader of *Leviathan*.

'Of Diligence and Jeopardy' reviews a modern-spelling edition of *Tyndale's New Testament, translated from the Greek by William Tyndale in 1534* (Yale University Press, 1989) and *The Revised English Bible with the Apocrypha* (Oxford University Press and Cambridge University Press, 1989), with references to the *Revised Standard Version* and the *New English Bible*. The connection is perfectly clear: 'The moral attitudes of the REB "team", or of those who address the world on its behalf, resemble those of the "group" responsible for the Second Edition of the *Oxford English Dictionary*' (p. 38), and Hill argues his case with some coruscating irony. In both instances, his argument is with the editorial posturing, and in the case of *The Revised English Bible* the actual translation which he characterises as 'not so much transmission as a kind of contamination' (p. 30). The intention of the Yale *Tyndale* is hardly controversial – to make Tyndale's work accessible – or original: it was Tyndale's own hope after all, and Biblical scholars since have worked hard to transmit his work, Hill's own favourite being Mombert's 1884 reprint. But Hill suggests that there 'is in fact an incompatibility between the Mombert and Yale editions which could be characterized as the difference between an old humility, not unworthy of Tyndale, and a new spirit of accommodation' (p. 23). Hill acknowledges the Yale editor's polemical stance against 'relevance' (p. 26), and his impatience with 'those whose main justification for the 1611 Bible is its status as "Sublime English Literature", "a particular glory of English letters", "the acme of achieveable literary perfection"' (pp. 29–30). But as Hill argues, 'You cannot, with equity, sneer at "Sublime English Literature" or pass judgement on "committees of people with no ears" if your own "hearing" permits the use of such phrases as "best-kept secrets in English Bible History", "the vivid, powerful, desert-wind intensity of much of Hebrew prophecy", "the bad press that Tyndale has had", "give us Tyndale any day" and "yet Tyndale can do equally well what Sir Walter Scott, in another context, called 'the Big Bow-Wow strain'"' (p. 30). That '"Tyndale's ravishing solo" must now be "heard across the world" as if he were some dissident poet in line for the Nobel Prize' (p. 27) identifies the pitch of Hill's anger. As he tellingly reminds us, in 1910 the Everyman Library brought out an edition of *The First and Second Prayer Books of Edward VI* in the original Tudor English. The editor of the text and J.M. Dent himself 'were not insensitive to the needs' of their wide readership, 'but like some other men of letters at that time, they showed respect for the intelligence of "ordinary" people by occasionally making demands upon it' (p. 39). 'To set the old Everyman text and introduction' (ibid) against the Yale *Tyndale* or *The Revised English Bible* 'is to begin to understand the irreparable damage inflicted, during the past ninety years or so, on the common life of the nation' (ibid). That 'damage' is excoriatingly exposed when Hill turns to the work of the 'team' (p. 34) responsible for *The Revised English Bible* and their hapless chairman Lord Coggan:

> When my wife and I celebrated our 40th wedding anniversary I bought her a piece of jewellery and I did *not* wrap it in newspaper.

So it is with the Bible – the greatest treasure of all must likewise be presented worthily (p. 35).

'Worthily' in this case seems to be entirely to do with accessibility and 'intelligibility' (p. 39) for 'the times we live in' (p. 34), but as Hill points out 'There is no end to the "demands" which the "times" will make. The "Age", in this, is like any other moral or emotional blackmailer' (ibid). Hill is forensic in his analysis of the shoddiness the concessions betray. When Coggan argues that, ' "The revision has been concerned to avoid archaisms, technical terms, and pretentious language as far as possible" ' (p. 36), Hill replies that 'This is specious syntax. An archaism can be historically determined and described by lexicography; a technical term can be defined; 'pretentious language', as used here, is a small balloon of prejudice and ignorant self-approval' (ibid). Even in their efforts to avoid such issues, the translators of both the REB and the infamous NEB prove their scholarly and literary ineptitude: the word 'diligent' being translated variously as 'you should make every effort', 'you should try your hardest', 'do your utmost to establish' and 'exert yourselves to clinch' (p. 42). The fact that the translators of *The Revised English Bible* sought advice from 'prominent literary figures such as the late Philip Larkin, the poet, and the novelist Mary Stewart' (p. 39) is almost as damning as the text itself, and they might have been better advised to heed the words of Karl Barth: 'The Gospel does not expound or recommend itself. It does not negotiate or plead, threaten, or make promises. It withdraws itself always when it is not listened to for its own sake' (p. 43).

The remaining five essays range narrowly but largely – to adapt Hill's own comment on Burton's lifetime at Christ Church – from Burton and Nashe to Hooker and Donne, from Vaughan and Hobbes to Herbert and Charles Wesley, and finally to Eliot's own exemplary response to the same centuries and writers. As always the arguments are meticulous with detail and discrimination, making it difficult to give a sense of the achievement. What holds them together is an interest in context, an interest indicated in the subtitle of Hill's previous collection of essays, *The Enemy's Country: Words, Contexture, and other Circumstances of Language.* In 'Keeping to the Middle Way,' Hill notes the significance of Robert Burton's 'It is most true, *stylus virum arguit*, our stile bewraies us, and as Hunters find their game by the trace, so is a mans *Genius* descried by his workes' (p. 45) for a historical moment when 'to leave such a trace can be dangerous, if not fatal' (p. 46). For Burton and other Anglican scholars and poets, 'The medium is best' (p. 47), the *via media* 'that Donne absorbed ... so deeply that it became the basis of his own thinking'

(p. 50). At least part of Burton's concern in *The Anatomy of Melancholy* is to analyse melancholia's 'monstrous capacity to hinder communion and fellowship' (p. 50). Burton achieves this with energetic humour, 'a parodist of "loose regarde" and a hunter of vulgar folly' (p. 53), for Hill standing halfway 'between two other great comedians: Shakespeare, of *A Midsummer Night's Dream*, and Hobbes, of "Apparitions or Visions" and "The Kingdome of Darkness"' (pp. 53–4), an achievement Hill delights in celebrating: 'The manner in which the huge, "loose", referential edifice of *The Anatomy of Melancholy*, the "confused company of notes writ with as small deliberation, as I doe ordinarily speak", can yet be so tellingly pointed and cadenced by one sentence – the simple authority of "In the name of Christ Jesus rise and walke" – is wonderful almost beyond words' (p. 64). Equally wonderful, in the same essay, is the interplay between context and words in Donne's 'Hymne to Christ, at the Author's last going into Germany,' where the phrase 'everlasting night' (p. 66) has sent so many Freudian scholars off in search of the lifelong death wish they think they also detect in *Biathanatos*'s '*Cupio dissolvi*, I desire to be dissolved and to be with Christ' (ibid). Hill obviously 'cannot disprove the claim that (Donne) suffered from a lifelong suicidal tendency' (ibid), but he can point out that the phrase quoted from *Biathanatos* 'is Pauline theology' (ibid), whilst acknowledging that for the seventeenth century reader ' "everlasting night" would surely strike eye and ear as a shocking spiritual oxymoron or wild aural pun' (ibid). As Hill argues, the phrase 'retorts upon "The Anniversarie", the celebration of love's "first, last, everlasting day", but inordinately so' (pp. 66–7), but part of the point of Hill's argument is that whilst he agrees with Helen Gardner's view that Donne completely 'absorbed Hooker's conception of the *via media*' (p. 50), and that ' "inordinate" is his characteristic pejorative … yet he himself inclines to the inordinate' (p. 65). The search for discriminations here is painstaking and beyond the reach of Freudians, precisely because the meaning is found in context and in metre and rhyme, an argument deepened in what Hill writes about Henry Vaughan.

'A Pharisee to Pharisees,' 'The Eloquence of Sober Truth', and 'The Weight of the Word' are as complex as the essays already discussed, and it is clearly beyond the range of a short review to do more than glance at such rich work. Context in 'A Pharisee to Pharisees' is the Commonwealth, the 'loud, evil days' (p. 74) of defeat for the Royalist and Anglican Vaughan, whose 'earthly Church of England had in fact vanished' (p. 77) by 1650. Knowing this, however, Vaughan's metaphysics ' "of deep, but dazling darkness"' (p. 85), and his ' "light-darkness opposition"' (ibid), make it 'reasonable to ponder what it is that draws or impels Vaughan' (p. 83) to the insistent night/light rhyming of 'The Night.' Campion,

Herbert, Wotton and Jonson all explore the apposition, but with Vaughan it clearly assumes 'ontological dimensions' (p. 81). Hill provides an exhaustive analysis, and placed in the context of the story of the Pharisee Nicodemus, visiting Jesus in the darkness to find the light, the significance for Vaughan is made obvious. 'The Eloquence of Sober Truth,' a review of *Early Responses to Hobbes*, is again an exploration of intention rather than etymology (p. 116), concentrating largely on Bramhall and Clarendon, in the context of Hooker's *The Lawes of Ecclesiasticall Politie* and the scholars writing after *Leviathan* and *De Cive*. 'Virtually without exception' (p. 93) the authors responding to Hobbes 'leave little room to doubt that language, in relation to private and public practice, is at the heart of the matter' (ibid), a 'matter' with serious implications ever since the 1559 Acts of Supremacy and of Uniformity when disputes over 'Supreme Head' or 'Supreme Governor' (p. 111) of the Church of England could have fatal consequences. As Hill notes, 'Despairing men are desperate men; desperate men are instant and armed desperadoes. At times, one feels, life-and-death decisions of state appear to be projections of the rhetorical figure *traductio*' (ibid). Christopher Morris's wry comment that 'among other "Elizabethan assumptions", "reason of state" was somehow different from normal reason' (ibid) sounds disturbingly familiar to modern ears. The penultimate essay in the volume, 'The Weight of the Word,' attends to Isabel Rivers's *Reason, Grace and Sentiment: A Study of the Language of Religion and Ethics in England 1660–1780. Volume 1: Whichcote to Wesley* (Cambridge University Press, 1991). Without having read Dr Rivers's work it is hardly possible to address Hill's reservations directly, but one finds the same issues of context explored. It does seem problematical 'to discuss Locke's civil and religious thought' (p. 119) in the two separate volumes when the context, in this example, is a single mind: Locke's. Similarly, even allowing for the fact that Dr Rivers's interest is 'the language of religious and moral prose' (ibid), it is difficult to quite see how one can understand Donne or Herbert or Vaughan's prose without studying their poetry. (The same, of course, is true of Hill himself.) Again, Hill is particularly acute in identifying the difference between Herbert's condescension to his unlettered seventeenth century flock in Bemerton (p. 133) and the circumstances which daily faced the 'Anglican, high Tory Wesleys' (ibid), and the effects these differing circumstances had upon their use of language. He also recognises 'the widespread emphasis, among theologians as well as scientists, on words as "arbitrary signs"' (p. 136), and how far we have journeyed towards 'an effusive post-Symbolism which coy and prurient exercises in the "confessional" mode have further dissipated' (p. 139).

To go from the sixteenth and seventeenth centuries to the 'Classicist,

Royalist, Anglo-Catholic' Eliot[1] is a way of acknowledging our own dilemma. 'Dividing Legacies' (first published in *Agenda*, summer 1996) reviews *The Varieties of Metaphysical Poetry: The Clark Lectures at Trinity College, Cambridge, 1926, and the Turnbull Lectures at the John Hopkins University, 1933*, edited and introduced by Ronald Schuchard (Faber, 1993). Eliot never published these lectures in his lifetime, and Hill argues a radical unease in Eliot with his own observation that ' "we have to consider the centre of gravity of metaphysical poetry to lie somewhere between Donne and Crashaw, but nearer the former than the latter" ' (p. 142). Part of the problem, for Hill, is Eliot's decision not to ' "draw in the background much more completely, with the figures of James, and Charles, and Hooker, and Laud, and Hyde and Strafford" ' (ibid), which Hill accounts as much a 'misjudgement' (ibid) as his 'miscalculation' (ibid) in pursuing 'the comparison and contrast with "Dante and his school" ' (ibid). Hooker is the essential figure here, and Hill again draws attention to Helen Gardner's recognition ' "that Donne has absorbed Hooker's conception of the *via media* so deeply that it has become the basis of his own thinking" ' (p 143). 'Dividing Legacies' analyses at depth the possible reasons for Eliot's failure, 'the final incoherence of the Clark Lectures' (p. 148), comparing the 'instinctively metaphysical' (p. 150) genius of the poet-critic in identifying Shakespeare's achievement in ' "It is well done, and fitting for a princess/Descended of so many royal kings./Ah, soldier!" ' (pp. 149–50) with the way 'Eliot's poetry declines over thirty years from pitch into tone' (p. 156): 'In "The Love Song of J. Alfred Prufrock" the distinction between I, me, my, we, us, our, you, your, his, her, they, them, one, it, its is a proper distinction in pitch; in "Little Gidding" communication is by tone' (p. 157) of which the 'residual beneficiaries … have been Larkin and Anglican literary "spirituality", two seeming incompatibles fostered by a common species of torpor' (pp. 158–59). The analysis is far too detailed to consider here, and Hill is emphatically not 'impugning the sincerity of Eliot's Anglo-Catholic devotion' (p. 158). But his 'argument does not require that we should be relieved of the office proper to our intelligence' (p. 157). That final salutary admonition is the proper function of criticism, as Eliot would well have recognised. *Style and Faith* is essential and exhilarating reading for anyone interested in literature and language.

[1] T.S. Eliot, 'Preface,' *For Lancelot Andrewes*, (Faber, 1927)

(Readers might like to recall: 'Geoffrey Hill Special Issue', Vol. 17 No. 1, Spring 1979; Vol. 23 Nos 3–4, 1985/86, a symposium of essays on Hill's *Collected Poems*; Vol. 30 Nos 1–2, Spring–Summer 1992, 'Geoffrey Hill Sixtieth Birthday Issue'.)

Rosemary Markham

The Sea and the Dog in the Poetry of Stephen Knight

In Stephen Knight's poetry, the dog outruns common sense. It is disturbing and doesn't fit tidily into ordinary life. It makes hectic dashes from organised life and races alone along the strand by the voluptuous sea, and crashes the waves. Through the dog symbol Knight sets going a fable about the creative impulse.

The dog represents unwilled levels of human personality. It deviates, doesn't stay true to type, like the poet himself. Knight, born in Swansea in 1960, 'slept on the ceiling with moths', was even called 'a dog ... showing us your teeth', apt to 'snarl in Chemistry'. Yet he was known for 'hooting like a seal ... moving like the tide'. Since 'a boy in captivity', he has been 'dreaming of the sea,' loosely illustrative of quest and enquiry, the dog in him 'racing along the strand'.

The motel in 'The Surf Motel' offers an ideal realm, albeit tedious with routine, but 'the cost of staying blurs on every bill.' This 'cost' is the cost of time a single life-span seems not enough and the poet has a horror of old age, of the impenetrable malice of the condition. Many poems bear on this. Sand measures time and in the haunting villanelle, 'The Desert Inn' in *Dream City Cinema* (Bloodaxe, 1996), he shows his fear: sand is 'at our door/ its progress through the keyhole slow:/ I raise both hands to hold it back before/ Sand pours towards me...'

In 'My Last Castle' in the moving collection *Sardines and Other Poems* (Young Picador, 2004) – ostensibly for the young but with a much wider appeal –the poet is building a sandcastle by the moon's light, the only sound his breath 'and the regiments of waves/ no-one in their right mind/ braves.' The waves of course devour his dream-castle, and 'walking back,/ I was lonely, yes, it's true,/ and saddened even then by what/ the sea is made to do.' The sea, aboriginal, impervious, obeys the moon.

He even feels at times 'trapped here, with the sea; you hear it whispering.' But he is compelled to follow and has stamina of response as well as heightened apprehension. He wades further in, against many warnings and 'The ocean bites...it chews and gnaws', – like a beast or the dog – yet he pushes on. Fear is linked to freedom. Feeling one, he feels the other. This one poem, 'Red Flag Lullaby', compresses the story of the poet enacting his own future.

Society, in all its directive powers, is intent on belittling the sea, and to Knight the city is profoundly unsympathetic. Swansea, which begot his sea poems, proved useful to the ordering of his thoughts into a robust perception of sea and city in collision. The city degrades itself through capitalism, technology and by life-style, leading to anonymity, conformity, delinquency and poor taste. To be 'Drifting on dry land' and 'crawling with cobwebs' is to be in the death domain.

Decadence is a colonising force. The sea, polluted literally, and in its metaphorical condition because few people now feel wonder, is yet in magnificent opposition as a life-giving force. The drama represents almost a development of the Soul/Body dialogues of old religious poetry. Formerly, the sea needed its debris, it pounded everything to sand; but such is the power of modern pollutants, that the sea is in peril. So it is that vestiges of the Soul still in the city – summed up in the dog who appears in another guise as a wild man in *The Sandfields Baudelaire* (Smith/Doorstep, 1996) – have a value beyond price. They are the link to life-renewing forces and unless they are respected, the city is into a slow suicide.

Sandfields is an area close to the sea in Swansea, on the Mumbles Road and Knight's collection, *The Sandfields Baudelaire*, looks like a Chinese wall of undigested vocabulary, the poems being cast in near unreadable, phonetically spelt Swansea speech. The collection has an underlying message: the man in the street may have valuable insights that run against the grain of today's popular culture although, like the dog, he is without a communicable language. The chief protagonist has something of Knight about him; he is mesmerised by the sea even in winter when there are 'clouds droppin' to our knees' and 'waves open up like a zip'. He suffers but he is aware that the sea suffers. True to character, here, he sees beauty in ugliness, but he also sees a terrifying question: 'Where will you spend Eternity?'

Knight has always had the capacity for self-criticism and when he is at his funniest he is usually at his most serious and self-deflating. In *Dream City Cinema*, he 'acquiesced in second best' like everyone else, being both juror and accused, a dual role characteristic of him, while he sat on the beach watching the waves 'deposit seven types of shit'. He is not a strategist, but, like the character in *The Sandfields Baudelaire*, he isn't dead to city degradation, nor to the power of the sea, that symbol of meditation on man and on matters beyond our ken. Like the old Welsh bards, he is a kind of seer, uses assonance, and like them has such a grasp of metre that, when he breaks from rhyme, it is hardly perceptible. Like the Welsh bards, too, he proclaims his judgements and his heroes, but with regard to the hero, it hits him late as to who the hero really is.

Free from inanities, Knight always wanted, like the dog, to be poised on the edge of difficult experience rather than kidnapped by propriety and the norms of city life. In youth he diverged from his parents who wanted to see him 'settled down'. He first flickered 'with the leaves and

72

the pages of my writing-pad like fire' when still in his father's care. Yet his father, a wireless operator during the war and near forty when Knight was born, who lived vicariously through cinema, fantasy and his boy, became Daedalus in the poem of that name. And the son, who saw himself as an often deluded Icarus, neither estranged nor drowned, was into a vexed flight: 'Doors/ Slam shut...Feathers falling everywhere'.

Yet it was his father who said, 'There's more to life than "Me Me Me"' in 'Notes for a poem called "Me Me Me"' in *Flowering Limbs* (Bloodaxe, 1993), a poem notable for its lack of focus which mirrored the poet's predicament at that time. The macabre line with which he shrugged the poem off: 'The oven, at a pinch, can hold three heads' represents himself and his parents from whom he felt mostly estranged.

It is years down the line before he sees that his father's loyal efforts, his ambience, even his admonitions as 'the shouting one', were threads in the web of natural affinities which he, the son, so respects. The father, in fact, was instrumental in waking a sleeping dog, a dog who, up to that point, had thought of himself as more awake than the waker.

In *Sardines and Other Poems*, Knight vividly and movingly recollects his father who died at the turn of this century. In 'Hide and Seek', he is watching himself, as is often his way, critically, yet here he is very conscious of his loss expressed without adornment: 'You are out alone, but no-one cares ... Your dad's nowhere in sight'. He cannot reconcile himself to his father's death, but he records his appreciation of his father's life to which *Sardines and Other Poems* is a tribute, establishing his father, perhaps ironically, as the real hero he sought.

Thus, if the dog represents unwilled levels of human personality, the sea which symbolises quest and inquiry also seems to represent the unconscious, instinctive levels in the psyche. It is to this sea, that oscillating edge of meditation, which Knight will no doubt return to inculcate its rhythms and to plumb its depths.

John Fuller

The Rivals

1. Sachs

Midsummer-day, the year's arch, is my name day.
Forever in the fullness of the year
Midsummer- and St John's day are the same day:
Johannestag, Johannes, Hans... My dear,
Do you remember picking chanterelles
Whose creamy buttons showed above the moss
Like liquid notes that float from the clear bells
Of oboes on a misty day across
A meadow? We were in the little wood
That's scattered down the stream, a place so haunted
It charmed us from ourselves so that we could
Discover who we were, so that you wanted
To rest there for a while, your shoulder on
My shoulder... And I am Hans, and not yet gone.

They grow where leaf-enhancing sunlight dapples
The mossy bank beside the talking stream,
Like apricots just stretching to be chapels
Or crumbling capitals of stone that dream
Of missing architraves. Loosed to your fingers
And light as pleated paper, into the basket
They twirl like trumpets. When the gatherer lingers
It is to seek a question, and then ask it:
What is the final form of our endeavours?
Is it to founder farthest from our faults?
To breast the wave that breaks, the arch that severs?
Or simply to set out, like these peach vaults
That leap up from the undemanding green
And do not care if they are never seen?

Across the emptiness that I am used to,
Something appears that's pointing to a place
That with a helping hand I'd be induced to
Leap to if I tried. It is your face,
Which asks in teasing silence if there is

74

Some simple reason why I live alone.
My eyes and tongue are mortal enemies.
Seeing and speaking are at odds. I own
A fatal gift for knowing how to wait,
For making the decisive move not cheerfully
Too soon, but overseriously, late;
Not with a reassuring smile, but tearfully,
As though I could not stretch across that void
Without one side or other being destroyed.

And after all, I would not wish to share
The empty life that sharing is designed
To fill. How could I come to you and stare
Into those willing eyes only to find
The blank reflection of my own disgust
At having nothing more to offer you?
And you? How long could you preserve your trust
In things that could not possibly be true,
Such as a purpose in the self-contained,
Feeling in the complacent, change in the old,
Or any wish to be unlike a pained
Observer of the tide of life, a cold
Unpenetrated heart of loneliness
Who's long moved on from his last known address?

That wild unsettled look is sprawled across
The squares of every life. Passing, you see
The zones of misery, the Martyr's Cross,
The selfish corners where a memory
Touches its grimy forelock for a drink,
The benches where the stiff mistakes nod on
Throughout an autumn's fury. Do you think
That love could ever change them? Would they be gone
After one season of your sweet patrol?
Sometimes I think they might. The clouds are blown
Across the moon in veils. The quietened soul
Sits of an evening on a still-warm stone
Within the hearing of a stream, while far
Above shines one bright unexpected star.

2. Beckmesser

My wicked comfort is that everyone
Knows what it's like: the ground pulled out from under
And all you thought you had achieved undone,
Reduced to stammering, a holiday wonder.
We each have this unique tremendous chance,
Luck carelessly worn, the gift of song,
The formula for love learned at a glance:
And then you realise you got it wrong.
But it is yours. Still is. You live with it,
This vast mistake committed without coercion.
The air is shaking with your lack of wit
And love's in shambles in your broken version.
Your whole life led to this derisive laughter.
This is where you stop. There's nothing after.

I don't trust them an inch. I know their ways.
Their sins define a civic history
That no remorse is able to erase,
And all are in my book. They have to be,
For I am Sixtus Beckmesser. I am
Town Clerk of Nuremberg. I write down all
That happens here. The bee, the oak, the lamb
Offer their services. In the Town Hall
Are deeds and registers, row upon row,
Room after room. The spider on the shelf
Knows everything a spider needs to know.
I am the Recording Angel. I am myself.
Nothing that's happened need have, nor will last
Unless I say so. I control the past.

It all comes to a preparation for
This moment. It gathers with proprietary
Fondness like a father at the door,
Hiding, to hear the ending of a story
That once when he was young he thought he knew.
It is the forbidden second chance of time.
It is the chalk scrawl of equations, true
At the proof. It is the undiscovered crime
That lies behind the questions of the present,
A history of expectation and

The characters of pleasant and unpleasant
Pieces in a game as yet unplanned
But somehow played already. It's a mad
Look at the future you've already had.

And then, the worst of failure is the thought
That no-one else considers it a sin
Simply to be yourself. It's you who's caught
By this killed promise of the might-have-been,
You who had secretly expected better
And you who even now, as mental editor
Of these events, reverse their upshot, debtor
And bankrupt turned to cheated creditor.
How-Could-I is the seed of It's-Not-True,
Ruined-Forever of Let's-Call-A-Halt.
You learn to claim that all the time you knew
It wasn't yours but circumstance's fault,
A chance that led you into wanting what
You scarcely hoped for, and then added: 'Not'.

Why did I think the song itself would win
And so make true the only thing which feeds it?
The unfulfilled desire where we begin
Is where we end: imagination needs it.
It is the only good for which we long,
It is the consolation of our age,
It is the master passion of our song,
The private reason for the public rage.
Better to steal, if stealing there must be,
To show your hunger all that it has lost.
Better learn feelings from the melody,
Considering the dignity it cost.
Passions run on and leave you far behind:
Each one of them is not the least you mind.

3. Sachs

Why did I think that love itself would win
And so create the only thing it makes?
Song is the beauty we are perfect in.
Song is the interest our self-loathing takes.
How can we claim desire at second-hand
Or offer prizes to unhappiness,
Lonely as ever when we take our stand
And closing palms mock with their loud address?
Better to give, if giving there must be,
The things that can be shared only in art
And soothe the feelings with new melody:
Better the rules are broken than the heart.
Songs will redeem our passions if we let them.
Songs are the means by which we can forget them.

And then the future: scanning the empty track,
Faint cries upon the dusky air, the tall
Competitors look forward. And look back.
You find yourself in motion after all.
Whose is that presence breathing at your side?
Whose is the daunting shape whose step you share?
The body's largest organ seems to stride
Like thunder over mountains, everywhere.
You sense that for a lifetime you must wait
For life to give the signal it's begun.
In what you always hope is the last straight
You give your all, and think the race is won:
Acknowledge that your true role was to pace
Your own performance, which will not take place.

The song is his, and somehow he conceived it
Out of an air electric with his urge
To be, and bring to being. He received it
As birthright, testimony, pledge. A surge
Of human recognition left him sick
Of incompleteness, sick of the consequence
And drift of all the studious rhetoric
That forms the life of dullness and expense.
And so the song required its object, not
To gratify, but to absolve, to bless.

78

Without that answering instruction, what
Could a garden be but a rich wilderness,
Nature's last joke, with nothing left to choose
Between a worldly mistress and the muse?

Happy enough to know that you are there:
Your love is like a pillar, a reprieve.
It is enough to last me. What we share
Sustains a future over which I grieve,
Knowing our sharing has a natural end:
Your life outstretching mine simply in years
Defines a dizzy breach too deep to mend,
Both wound and weapon, fantasy and fears.
I see it waiting for you, undefined
Except as waiting. Like some wayward sprite
Looking to occupy a vacant mind
With haunting of a sort. And so it might,
Once it's invited there to take its chance
In the charmed wastefulness of ignorance.

The moon still hangs upon the morning hill
As if it had been blanched into a skull
Through night's dead influence. I see it still,
That mossy bone, that socket, that pale hull
Beached in the daylight on the travelling sky,
The doomed adventurer of all our dreams,
The false associate whose credible lie
Haunts our imaginings with borrowed beams.
No, it is not the sun. But very soon
I know I'll feel that massive warmth behind me.
Westward I'm gazing still, to keep the moon
Within my sight, but soon the sun will find me.
And it will shine, as yesterday it shone
Unstintingly. The moon will soon be gone.

Two Chosen Broadsheet Young Poets:

Sinead Wilson
and Ailie Macdonald

Sinead Wilson is 31 and was born, brought up and currently lives in South London. She is Head of Media Studies at Plumstead Manor School in South-East London. Her work has appeared in *Reactions 5*, *PN Review* and *North*, and has been anthologised.

The Downs

The bed rears above us –
our Beachy Head,
a white cliff of mattress
down to a Paisley carpet sea;
aroused, you turn seal
navigating cold water, restless.

A boat without mooring,
I keel, shifting on the current;
a wind floods the sail's breast,
crimps the weft about us.
The boat shaves closer to the rocks –
far-off storms are coming into shore.

You resurface, catch breath,
before returning down.
Our octopus child wakes empty
in the next door room,
her skirt anchored to a toy:
silent, one eye blinking in the dark.

The Engineers

Wet afternoons, one of us would turn Mickey Rooney
and plan to stage our own Broadway musical
right here against the garden fence,
or suggest we build a Dalek in the back room
from egg boxes and black poster paint.

We had designs grand as Paxton or Bazalgette,
the bedroom library, the bathroom museum
- its sole exhibit a desiccated seahorse,
The art gallery on Daniel's stairs of pictures
we had drawn ourselves and one of Fonzy from a jumble sale.

I loved the excitement of the schemes but lost all hope
when things would pan out wrong or not be beautiful enough,
as when we made the angel wings from twigs
and candle wax but had to stop when all that soft white down
refused to stick and turned into a greasy mush.

The Human Thermometer

Slurping cocoa from a tablespoon,
he sat out afternoons in his captain's chair.
Trousers held up with a knotted tie,
he told me how, once, when he was five,
snowflakes billowed out in June,
large and white as pillow down.
Bedtime, I listened as he read
from *Amazons Forever*, bound by
a drum skin of army surplus blankets, sheets.
He took down a photo framed above my bed,
a bistre crowd of thirties boys
and helped me pick him out with cries
of *warmer, warmer, burning hot*
– my fingers scorching faces of the dead.

Ailie Macdonald is 18 and spent the first 11 years of her life in Perthshire. She is now studying for her A levels at Collyer's College in Horsham, Sussex and is going on to study English at degree level.

The Hierophant

Eight days at the bottom of the ocean –
The memory becomes sand
Storm surge beating
Cloven hooves upon your brow.
To the north

Snowdrifts melt too late,
The noise of the water above
Passing feet that shuffle dirty papers
To collect in archways
By gunshot walls in Alexanderplatz.

On the ninth, we rise; masters
Of the headlong waves,
Bright-eyed colts on a grey day.

Minos has confronted his Minotaur,
Each ungripped prong
A whiskered trumpet –
The ghost of scarlet daffodils,
One sullen eye aimed towards his heart.

The streets become motionless
In turbulence; steadfast refractions
Irreversible
Constant convections
Slowed
To freeze-framed mirrors
– Grace, heavenly rebirth in an ellipse.

Entangled in the severed reins
The crowd jeers feigned sympathy to the hero
The last of our royal and ancient house
Is lost;
The name is blotted out forever.

Hollow hills

Up-lit evening as the petals closed
Where were you?
Starling eyelids that close on the land
Embankments of feathered stone
Hesitating; leaning in on every growing space.

Your reluctance, soft resistance against the greying day
The gentle touch, that could make the sky fall
Into far-off starlit bays.
Hold this crest of light, thaw these tendrils of glass
That bind our eyes, our hearts.

Find the stony walls of your tumbledown Mountain;
Shelter among pebbledash thorns
Sharpened tin, and the cold stillborn.
Heat the walls and
Watch your ancestors climb through the haar.

Voices lost in amphitheatres long overgrown
Crowd round your broadleaf hands,
Shambling stories that barely cover the gaps
Retold by castaway days – threadbare ends
To catch the sweet dregs of the morning tide.

Our paths, widow fingers; that for so long ran parallel
Became lost and then, converged
In some knotty confluence rising high
Above this twilight's veiled cockle shells,
Between the bloom of this shadow and the next.

Sister's dress is folded, torn – she leads me to a clearing
Where crimson butterflies dance
Their crinkle-wings warming autumn light:
One hundred and fifty thousand
Or more, lapping saltwater from your open wounds.

The panic was lost on your half turned face,
As they circle
Quivering bodies brush against eyelids

As they circle
Chiffon dresses move under lamplight
As they circle

Insect wings fill the empty bedclothes,
As they circle
And fall into darkness.

Ageing

The days stack up:
Pears, Plums and Clam and cockleshell
Suitcase leathered, chalked.

It's getting colder,
Perhaps we should have told her.

A quiet that falls to numbered,
Branching creak-dry pines
After they have fallen
Under mildew steel, softened iron
In its death – a growing thing
All spores and rattling moss.
Red funeral dress
Red lace
Two wrists, clotted soil in eyelash.
Under the hull of some upturned boat
Under sky, under pinewood and mist,
Whispers of next year's pains.

It never stops getting colder
Perhaps we should have told her.

Shrill elevation – timed to
Hold our faces in these waters,
Deep and cold.
Far below, a broken summer
That ended every season.
Her hair – growing darker in the winter
Like hillside heather.

Eyes I wish were mine
Lions' yawn at sun-up
Watchful, over the gate at Mycenae
Old beggar man chews
On vulture wing.

Their stone-dust eyes were cautious
Till we moved away,
And under,
To creep at night through stolen shades
And stalk by long redundant palisades.

Broadsheet 6 is online
www.agendapoetry.co.uk

Notes for Broadsheet Poets 6

Journals are inspiring, intimate and accessible, offering keys to their authors. Gide, Kafka, Virginia Woolf, Yeats et al. wrote journals, both for public and private consumption, that intrigue, whether in diary, essay or letter forms. In them can be discovered the seeds of the creative impulse, secrets revealing the concerns and craft of writing, the climate of the day, even personal confessions.

Earlier in this series of **Notes for Broadsheet Poets** (available in *Agenda* and online), for example, Rainer Maria Rilke's 'Letters to a Young Poet' were cited, as were Yeats' Letters to Dorothy Wellesley. Each of these groups of 'Letters' comprises a kind of 'Poet's Journal', containing advice and tips for young poets. Another particularly relevant and startlingly articulate discovery is the **'Poet's Journal'** of **Pádraic Fallon**, the highly respected Irish poet and verse dramatist, born in 1905, whose *Collected Poems* were published by Carcanet in 1990. Fallon asks the very question that *Agenda*'s present editor has asked regarding the 'young' **Broadsheet** poets: 'What is a young writer? And what is an old writer?' As was suggested in the first **Notes for Broadsheet Poets**, a poet can be a 'young poet' at eighty if he has just started writing poetry and found his voice. Or, as Fallon cites, 'Yeats was a young man at seventy, Higgins was old at forty.'

In *A Poet's Journal & Other Writings 1934–1974*, edited by Brian Fallon and published by The Lilliput Press in 2005, Fallon's timeless poetic credo or testament can be found. This comprises ten instalments written from September 1951 to November 1952, for the well-known journal *The Bell*. This lively, at times contentious, eccentric, poetic credo or 'Journal', is written in a chatty, accessible, even ironic witty style. Refreshingly, Fallon is never obsequious and has the guts to write off Eliot, Pound and Yeats at various stages in their careers before restoring them in part to their pedestals, e.g. 'Pound's Cantos were built to express the whole vision of the poet by using all his material. In that they were successful. He uses an art-form in which he can be mythic and moronic in the same space of a line. He can be stately and slummy, cryptic, gnomic and diffusive on the one page.' A little later he adds: 'When Pound started eating up continents, from Chicago to Cathay, Marc Apollo circling the globe, well, he needed a way to disgorge his giant eating, something so formless that it must be a form in itself, a book that has eaten up all the books.' In general, though, the Journal not only registers Fallon's poetic and dramatic principles as he struggles for a constructive synthesis; it also represents a guide to younger, fledgeling Irish poets. In it are real gems.

Fallon's allegiance about which he was not dogmatic, as Brian Fallon recounts in his introduction to *A Poet's Journal & Other Writings*, 'was to an imagistic type of poetry, with its roots in Symbolism but also in the Elizabethans and Metaphysicals; the type of quasi-journalistic verse that became popular from the thirties onwards seemed to him to compromise fatally with prose thinking and prose logic'.

As is the tradition in *Agenda*, and as evidenced above, Fallon challenges fashionable cults and idols with his risqué, incisive comments, describing fashion as 'the merest commonplace', adding a wisecrack: 'The clique always stands for a cliché.' Like *Agenda*, too, he reviewed and encouraged the early work of such poets as Ted Hughes, Elizabeth Jennings, Philip Larkin, and Thomas Kinsella. Fallon also showed considerable interest – after he was an active reviewer – in the early work of, among others, Seamus Heaney, Michael Longley and Eavan Boland, before he died in 1974.

It is hoped that the following quotations by this spirited magus startle, inspire, inform, enlighten and amuse as they add to the eternal cultural debate. I think Fallon would be delighted today for his profound musings and questions to arouse strong reactions whether of agreement, disagreement, intellectual ruminations, or applause...

From *A Poet's Journal II*:

What is poetry anyway? A display of personality or a vision of reality? Can it be both in one poem?

What then about yourself? Will you chuck the stanza-trunks and walk naked?

From *A Poet's Journal III*:

...The mystic way of speech is returning, the art of double and treble meanings, the concentration on the image, the variety and individuality of theme, good writing.

Words. Poems are written with them. Not with soul, not with spirit. With words. Mallarmé.

Poetry is made of words, said Mallarmé. But a poem is a series of continuous and immediate inspirations, one word borrowing another, and the poet has not very much choice about them. He will use the words that strike matches in his Unconscious, when he has them; he will use others disdainfully to plug holes when he hasn't, going back again to find the right ones later, the misfires.

I had to treat this country as if it was in my mind, that is, as it had come to me through folksong and folktale, and as I had lived it in fair and market, in town and country, a boy amongst his own people, who was lucky enough to have contacted the last remnants of the old Gaelic-speaking life and felt it reflected in the attitude of the community. Why, I used to holiday in houses where one man would recite Raftery's poems to another, where a boycotted landlord used to pass by under the protection of sweating policemen, where the Land War was still a real thing, where men working in a field would run a mile to see a horse gallop, where eighteenth-century recklessness lasted well into my time at fairs and race-meetings, where beggars talked John Millington Synge, and every man was an individual, the big house in the background dying into inanition. The Ireland of my youth connected me historically with the eighteenth century, but it was an emotional connection too, a joy in just living, in delighting in active things, in kicking up, like a young colt, one hell of a dust.

There is more to life than the despair of life. There is this body-joy in its own energies... There is measure and number in all things, but you discover them through excess.

A man takes his body from his parents, but his psyche is all man's. He is the history of the world. All times in all men.

Man's relations with the Gods are never out of date. They have the inner relevance of a neurosis. Complexes of urge and energy...

From *A Poet's Journal IV*:

Every writer knows his vocation from his schooldays and his attitude towards the world is born in him. It is the spirit-skeleton within the skeleton, and all his urge is to get this plain to himself... One's philosophy of life, indeed, consists of a long series of revulsions, each revulsion being a broken marriage of some kind or other. We skin-strip till we find the skeleton...

Most poets consider their own stuff the best there is, and all their criticism is consciously or unconsciously a propaganda for their own kind of poetry... If we accept a critic's job at all, we have to allow for personal bias and for one's own indecent motives.

No poet is ever a settled man; daily he builds his psyche anew, his everyday world, and it is a truism that one poet stimulates another to the building.

There is a daily logic somehow in the visual things the day presents, and if we kill the eye we see ourselves no better for being blind. Even in verse, if we do not bring things to the visual point, if we do not stamp words with the prints of things, we lose in direct strength and challenge.

The visual, however, is neither the real nor the realistic, but a help to communication, a lighting along the pathway that leads into the image. All good poetry must end in the image, and the image is a complex made visible, the end and the all.

Each poem is different from any other and demands its own kind of language and approach, demands and enforces it, indeed, and a poem fails only when the poet does not follow the poem faithfully in the kind of language it wants from him. To do that he must kill the idea of style, of one personal style, which was about the only serious limitation that Yeats had since it confined him to subjects that lent themselves to lordly utterance.

From *A Poet's Journal V*:

I believe that no poem of any use is ever made without some degree of possession, and when a poet is in that state he is something else than himself.

Whatever it is, it is dependent on the poet for its temporary expression, for its time-body, and the poet is dependent also upon it, for the words that well up from line to line, for the integrated passion of the utterance. I am tired of people who look on writing as a mere craft, but not as weary of them as of those who regard the writer's voice as the voice of God.

A Pre-Raphaelite doctrine, maybe. Emotion is everything... The best example could be Dante who made poetry out of his ruin, or Baudelaire, who lived ruin in order to feel it, de Nerval who went mad that he might know emotion from the other side of things, all the eccentrics of life who were forced to dramatise an attitude so that they could feel, so that they could feed that abstract person within with the passions of life. And poor Pound, escaping from it all his life, to be caught up by it at last in a cage-camp in Italy.

So my feeling is that a man is a projection in time of a personality outside time, a dual thing that could work each way, and while I needn't believe in this with the absoluteness of a doctrine, I can use it as most poets use any doctrine, as a working hypothesis, as fuel in the stove, as the negative and positive currents that come together in the bulb and throw some light into the room. Even Euripides, who scanted the Gods, was aware of other worlds.

And how much of feeling is suggestion? When I ask myself this, the void around me gapes. I question my own authenticity. I am confronted, like Baudelaire, with the horror of emptiness. And that itself is an emotion...

It is this up-against-it feeling that does make us creators, make us turn on special aspects of living so that the heart beats again.

The thing about form is that there comes a time when it becomes formal. Then it controls thought rather than releases it, and pens the poet in a convention.

Form, of course, is always necessary. Some subject, indeed, will demand a rigid scheme or there will be a stumbling and a halting and a churning all over the place, and a consequent loss in rhythmic value.

And the rhythm is the thing, the undercurrent and undertow that counterpoise the onward rush. But the learned stanza carrying its rhymes like airs and graces has ceased, I think, to be part of our time and makes me think of something I read somewhere in Proust's occasional writings. He said that initially the great inventors of art in the nineteenth century were all regarded as vulgar by the public, no matter how the critics stressed their contacts with the artists who went before them. They had to lower the expression to compete with the changing psyche.

The poet's obscure vision of reality, indeed, is never apparent to himself until he is getting it into words. Then the battle is joined. And in the queerest way he must yield up the greater part of his brilliant equipment, discard his facility and his dictionary, throttle his eloquence, and kill a thousand metaphors, if he is to find that something new that makes his hair stand up with triumph. If he takes the easy way of his facility, he will substitute something else for his actual vision....

I look for the VISION.

From *A Poet's Journal VI*:

...For most of us it is the suffering of matter that makes us speak, an ancient consciousness that we have as our first mission to transmit the cry of things beyond ourselves. Man is mythic not logical, Aeschylean and not Socratic, and when Plato burned his poems and founded his optimistic god on syllogisms of sophistries he gave us the university of the atom bomb.

All men, indeed, aspire naturally to the condition of art, for the problem of the duality of the world is solved, not by a logic, but by an aesthetic. There is neither good nor evil in the poetic cry, there is only a singleness, an acceptance of the haphazard will that inhabits the universe...

...The significances of myth are always with the poet, always in the poet. And whatever redactions of primeval feelings were in the gods are still active and move through us in metaphor and image. It is our job to give those currency, and in a Socratic world make them available to feeling again.

I have never spoken in a language I trusted. I have always necessarily upholstered myself with the properties of communication, as if I were an American footballer taking the field. All modern art is a compromise, and the poet wears a fleece so that he may walk with the flock.

The essence of an art is to the whole. And that is the trouble. The wholeness eludes us. We are the poets of fragments, our apparatus always out of order.

Il y a dans l'acte de l'amour une grande resemblance avec la torture ou avec une opération chirurgicale.

Those eternal mirrors of the modern man, this broken sensibility that sees itself by contraries. We constantly find ourselves in the arms of our opposites. We find our faith only by denial of it, as if the denial itself were a declaration of faith. And yet it is this kind of art we have to use if we are to get at the truth in ourselves and leave it free to affect others, a kind of truth by self-deception. There is no plain speech, there is only a large reading between the lines.

From *A Poet's Journal VII*:

Poetry should renew itself in every decade by refining itself from those impurities of time and place which give it a kind of temporary body in current taste... There is no such thing as pure poetry. There is a soul and a body in all things, the ideal form and its earth equivalent; but the earth form must alter in time and space and it is through this earth form that the ideal must speak to us. That is the current language of art; and like any other language it is always in the course of amending its meanings.

In admitting everything to our verse, we lessen the formal value of the statement. We forget we speak of the permanent and *for* the permanent. We intrude ourselves, that current Selfhood which most of the poets of the past distinguished from the identity, from the *moi profonde*, from the timeless soul. This soul is the poet's concern. And the revelation of it must be his art.

Nothing can exist in art as it exists in life. The artist connects one to the other. He is the meeting point at which they contemplate one another, two imponderables making mystic marriage, a poet making a poem. But because a poet must use a language which is abstracted from a current vocabulary and which must keep all the hints of its original if it is *to satisfy a man who speaks for his own time*, most poems cease to be poetry after a couple of generations of use. They 'fade on the page', as Robert Graves says: only the permanent continues its life, that thing in which the extraneous elements were least and the poet's time-body the least emphatic. The history of poetry is a history of lost causes and spent emotions, high indignations and high horses equally dust. What carries a poem is its language; the meaning that oozes through words like so much many-coloured oil is a matter of sound and syllables and nothing commonsensical that may be determined by any prose-précis.

A poem will find a poet.

One of Rilke's secrets, for instance, is that he brings forward the abstract noun into the foreground so that the foreground is thinned to a gauze, the poem, then, becoming a series of perspectives that run away back into some infinity, 'l'éternité qui gronde à l'horizon, la destiné où la fatalité qu'on apperçoit intérieurement sans qu l'on puisse dire à quelles signes on la reconnaît!' Realism has the pictorial appeal, but as Yeats said long ago, leave it to the painter.

A young poet seeks a philosophy but finds an aesthetic if he is lucky. It is a critic's job to insist on the difference.

From *A Poet's Journal VIII*:

What a poet is really after, indeed, is that extra dimension, the God; and the trouble is that the lyric genius and the mechanical so seldom come together.

(Printed by kind permission of Ivan Fallon.)

Biographies

Peter Abbs is Professor of Creative Writing at the University of Sussex. He is the author of seven volumes of poetry, including most recently *Viva la Vida* published by Salt in 2005. His polemic against Post-Modernism, *Against the Flow*, has been recently published by RoutledgeFalmer.

Gary Allen comes from Ballymena, Co. Antrim, Northern Ireland. He has had several collections published and his poems have been published widely in magazines and journals in Ireland and in the UK.

William Bedford has published poetry in *Agenda, Critical Quarterly, Encounter, The Independent, The Malahat Review, The Poetry Review, Poetry Salzburg Review, The Southern Review, The Washington Times* and many others. His novel *Happiland* was shortlisted for the Guardian Fiction Prize. He has received awards from the Arts Council and the Society of Authors.

David Betteridge has been writing poems for more than forty years, and publishing for less than five, in *Acumen, Anon, Cencrastus, Freedom Spring, Poetry Scotland*, and *Pulsar*. His inspiration has been drawn from both music and from poetry that shows a concern for the musicality of language, including works by David Jones and Basil Bunting.

Rob Blaney was born in Nantwich, Cheshire, in 1952. His poems have appeared in *Iota, Envoi, Raw Edge, The New Writer*, and as accompanying poems to books of short stories. He has undertaken readings in Australia and in the north-west of England. He is Chair of a writers' group and is keen to promote the work of young writers. By profession he works for a housing association.

Ian Caws's current collection is *Taro Fair* (Shoestring Press). *The Canterbury Road* is due from Bluechrome this year.

Martin Cook was born in India in the 1930s. His butterfly career included soldiering, tea planting, international marketing and social services. Retired to write poetry. Poems in over forty magazines including *Acumen, Ambit, Chapman, Envoi, Orbits, Other Poetry, Staple* and *Tears in the Fence*. He had one poem in *Agenda* years ago.

D.V. Cooke was born in Cheshire, England. He graduated in English from London University and worked for a number of years for the Poetry Library in London. He has published in numerous poetry magazines including: *Poetry Wales, Orbis, Stand and Babel*.

Greg Delanty is the Artist in Residence at St Michael's College, Vermont. He is politically active and ran for The Green Party in the US elections. His most recent books are *The Ship of Birth* (Carcanet Press 2003), due from LSU Press 2007, *The Blind Stitch* (Carcanet and LSU Press) and *The Hellbox* (Oxford University Press 1998). His *Collected Poems 1986–2006* is just out from Carcanet Press. He thanks Liam Ó'Muirthile for his help with O'Ríordáin's translations.

Martin Dodsworth taught English at Royal Holloway, University of London, for many years. He was associated with *the review*, and reviewed poetry in *The Guardian* for almost twenty years. He edited *The Survival of Poetry* (1970).

June English, born 1936 in Dover, Kent, read English and History as a mature student at the University of Kent, followed by an MA in Humanities. Her first collection, *Counting The Spots* (Acumen, 2000), was shortlisted for the BBC *New Voices* programme. *The Sorcerer's Arc*, her first full collection, was published by Hearing Eye in 2005. She founded the Dover and Deal 'Split the Lark Poetry Festival' in 1999.

Janice Fixter has a D.Phil. in Creative Writing from Sussex University. She has written books and articles on parenting and her poems have appeared in many poetry magazines. Her latest pamphlet is *Walking the Hawk* (Tall Lighthouse 2005) and she is currently working on a new collection due out in 2007. She lives in South London.

John Fuller's latest volume of poems, *Ghosts* (Chatto and Windus) was shortlisted for the Whitbread Prize. His novel *Flawed Angel* was published last year, also by Chatto. His poem 'The Rivals' will appear in a new collection to be entitled *The Space of Joy*. He has recently been awarded the Michael Braude Prize of the American Academy of Arts and Letters. He is an Emeritus Fellow of Magdalen College, Oxford.

Owen Gallagher is a primary teacher in Southall. *Sat Guru Snowman* was published by Peterloo Poets in 2001. He has received awards from The London Arts Board and The Society of Authors and won first prize in the Smurfit, Samhain, International Poetry Competiton, 2004.

John Greening's last collection was *The Home Key* (Shoestring). He has recently published studies of Yeats and First World War Poets with Greenwich Exchange. His next critical book will be about American poetry since 1963; his next collection of poetry is the result of a Society of Authors travel grant which took him to Iceland. He reviews for the TLS. His new website is www.johngreening.co.uk

Nicholas Jagger is a poet and artist whose work has previously appeared in *Agenda*, *Stand* and *HQ*.

Nigel Jarrett is a poet, essayist and short-story writer and a winner of the Rhys Davies Memorial Award for contemporary short fiction. Currently a freelance journalist, he has been music critic of the *South Wales Argus* daily newspaper since the late 1980s. His work appears widely and is in recent issues of *Planet*, *Poetry Wales*, *The Salisbury Review*, *The Black Mountain Review* (*Ulster*) and *Envoi*.

Michael Kirkham, born and educated in England, has lived and worked in Canada since 1968. He is Professor Emeritus in English at the University of Toronto. His books include *The Poetry of Robert Graves* (1969), *The Imagination of Edward Thomas* (1986), and *Passionate Intellect: The Poetry of Charles Tomlinson* (1999).

Kim Lasky is a D.Phil student in Creative and Critical Writing at the University of Sussex researching relations between poetry and criticism in contemporary writing and working towards a first collection.

Mark Leech's most recent book of translations, *Anglo Saxon Voices*, is published by Pipers' Ash Ltd. He won the Stephen Spender prize for poetry in translation in 2004, and has had poems published in a wide range of magazines. He lives in Oxford.

Isobel Lusted lives in London. She has published poems in several magazines and is a Keats/Shelley prizewinner.

Rosemary Markham has taught English Literature in various Colleges and for a brief time in the Open University. She writes on artists, reviews poetry, and writes general articles, recently on Cicely Hey for *The Burlington Magazine*.

Keith McFarlane lives and works in Amsterdam. Several of his poems have been published in *Acumen*.

Anita Money read English at St Hugh's College, Oxford. She was Editorial Assistant and Treasurer for *Agenda* in the 1990s. She guest-edited Vol. 35 No. 4– Vol. 36 No. 1 of *Agenda* in 1998. She is currently working in an inner city school.

Lawrence Sail has published nine collections of poems, most recently *Eye-Baby* (Bloodaxe Books, 2006). In 2005 Enitharmon brought out *Cross-currents*, a collection of his essays. He received a Cholmondeley Award in 2004.

Myra Schneider's most recent collection is *Multiplying The Moon* (Enitharmon 2004). Also recent is *Writing My Way Through Cancer*, a fleshed-out journal with poems (Jessica Kingsley 2003). She is co-editor of *Images of Women* (due autumn 2006), an anthology of women's poetry which is partly Arts Council funded.

Alex Smith, who lives in Saffron Walden, Essex, won the New Essex Writing Competition in 1993 and the Blue Nose Poets-of-the-Year Competition in 2001. He has published two full volumes of poetry including *The Appetites of Morning*, the *Languor of Afternoons* (1996, Salzburg University) and *Kayserling* (1997, Oversteps Press, Salcombe).

Gerard Smyth was born in Dublin and has been contributing to poetry in Ireland, Britain and North America since the 1960s. He has published five collections, including *Daytime Sleeper* (Dedalus, 2002) and *A New Tenancy* (Dedalus, 2004).

John Torrance is a retired university lecturer living in Poole who has been writing poetry for the past fifteen years, published mainly in *South, Tears in the Fence* and *Magma*.

Lynne Wycherley was recently selected as an Alternative Generation Poet (*Staple*). Her new collection *North Flight* charts a lyrical journey from the Fens to Orkney, Shetland and Iceland (Shoestring Press, autumn 2006). A further selection of her work features in *Into the Further Reaches: An Anthology of Contemporary British Poetry Celebrating the Spiritual Journey* (PSAvalon, Nov 2006, ed. Jay Ramsay).